Apple Pro Training Series
Compressor 3.5

Brian Gary

Apple
Certified

Apple Pro Training Series: Compressor 3.5
Brian Gary
Copyright © 2010 by Brian Gary
Published by Peachpit Press. For information on Peachpit Press books, contact:
Peachpit Press
1249 Eighth Street
Berkeley, CA 94710
(510) 524-2178
www.peachpit.com
To report errors, please send a note to errata@peachpit.com.
Peachpit Press is a division of Pearson Education.

Apple Series Editor: Serena Herr
Project Editor: Nancy Peterson
Development Editor: Bob Lindstrom
Production Coordinator: Kim Wimpsett, Happenstance Type-O-Rama
Technical Editor: Christopher Phrommayon
Copy Editor: Darren Meiss
Compositor: Craig W. Johnson, Happenstance Type-O-Rama
Indexer: Valerie Perry
Cover Illustration: Kent Oberheu
Cover Production: Happenstance Type-O-Rama

ISBN 13: 978-0-321-64743-6
ISBN 10: 0-321-64743-2
9 8 7 6 5 4 3 2 1
Printed and bound in the United States of America

Contents at a Glance

Table of Contents

Getting Started

Welcome to the official Apple Pro training course for Compressor 3.5, Apple's digital distribution hub for Final Cut Studio. This book is an in-depth reference for encoding with Compressor. It covers the use of Batch Templates, Droplets, Frame Controls, Job Actions, and Filters. It also illustrates advanced features such as custom settings, third-party plugins, and integration with other Final Cut Studio applications.

Whether you're an expert compressionist or encoding media for the first time, Compressor's simple workflows will quickly have you publishing for iPods and iPhones, DVDs, Blu-ray Discs, and Internet destinations such as YouTube and MobileMe. You will also learn post-production techniques for film and video workflows.

System Requirements

Before using *Apple Pro Training Series: Compressor 3.5,* you should have a working knowledge of your Macintosh and the Mac OS X operating system. Make sure that you know how to use the mouse, and standard menus and commands; and also how to open, save, and close files. If you need to review these techniques, see the printed or online documentation included with your system.

For the basic system requirements of Compressor 3.5, refer to the Final Cut Studio documentation, or Apple's website, www.apple.com/finalcutstudio.

About the Apple Pro Training Series

Apple Pro Training Series: Compressor 3.5 is a reference aid, a self-paced learning tool, and the official curriculum of the Apple Pro Training and Certification Program. Developed by experts in the field and certified by Apple, the series is used by Apple Authorized Training Centers worldwide and offers complete training in all Apple Pro products. The lessons are designed to let you learn at your own pace. The book's online companion page, www.peachpit.com/apts.compressor, includes review questions and answers summarizing what you've learned, which can be used to help you prepare for the Apple Pro Certification Exam.

For a complete list of Apple Pro Training Series books, see the ad at the back of this book, or visit www.peachpit.com/apts.

Apple Pro Certification Program

The Apple Pro Training and Certification Program is designed to keep you at the forefront of Apple's digital media technology while giving you a competitive edge in today's ever-changing job market. Whether you're an editor, graphic designer, sound designer, special-effects artist, or teacher, these training tools are meant to help you expand your skills.

Upon completing the course material in this book, you can become a certified Apple Pro by taking the certification exam at an Apple Authorized Training Center. Certification is offered in Compressor, Final Cut Pro, Motion, Color, Soundtrack Pro, DVD Studio Pro, and Logic Pro. Successful certification as an Apple Pro gives you official recognition of your knowledge of Apple's professional applications while allowing you to market yourself to employers and clients as a skilled, pro-level user of Apple products.

For those who prefer to learn in an instructor-led setting, Apple offers training courses at Apple Authorized Training Centers worldwide. These courses, which use the Apple Pro Training Series books as their curriculum, are taught by Apple Certified Trainers and balance concepts and lectures with hands-on labs and exercises. Apple Authorized Training Centers have been carefully selected and have met Apple's highest standards in all areas, including facilities, instructors, course delivery, and infrastructure. The goal of the program is to offer Apple customers, from beginners to the most seasoned professionals, the highest-quality training experience.

For more information, please see the ad at the back of this book, or to find an Authorized Training Center near you, go to training.apple.com.

Resources

Apple Pro Training Series: Compressor 3.5 is not intended as a comprehensive reference manual, nor does it replace the documentation that comes with the application. For more information about Compressor, refer to these sources:

▶ Compressor User Manual—Accessed through the Motion Help menu, the User Manual contains a complete description of all the features.

▶ Apple's website—www.apple.com.

▶ Peachpit's website—Online review questions and answers, which can be used to help you prepare for the Apple Pro Certification Exam, can be found at this book's companion webpage: www.peachpit.com/apts.compressor.

1

Core Concept   Learn the basic functions of Compressor's five main windows

Compressor Basics

Digital media distribution has become both varied and multifaceted. Long gone are the days when laying your final edit out to tape was the only option. Now you may find yourself producing video screeners for iPods and iPhones, compressing movies for Apple TV playback, encoding high-quality trailers for YouTube, and creating both DVDs and Blu-ray Discs. Modern post-production workflows involve cross-compatibility between video and audio files in many different formats, and between the hardware platforms used to create and manipulate them. Compressor shines as the digital distribution hub for work inside Final Cut Studio, and for the other platforms in your post-production pipeline.

Fortunately, you can use Compressor as either a beginner or advanced user. For the beginner, the batch template workflows described in Lesson 2 produce high-quality, distributable media and require very little encoding knowledge. The advanced user can dig deeply into Compressor's encoding settings, harness its batch management and monitoring capabilities, and increase its speed and efficiency using distributed encoding.

Compressor uses five main windows to guide you through the different steps of the encoding process: the Batch window (with Batch Template Chooser), the Preview window, the History window, the Inspector window, and the Settings window.

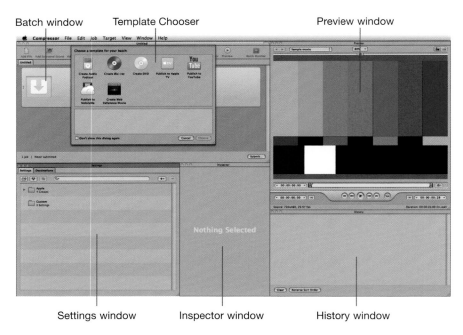

Compressor's Standard window layout

Standard Window	Function
Batch window	The vast majority of work done in Compressor starts and finishes inside the Batch window. Templates are accessed, media is imported, targets are applied, destinations are selected, output filenames are customized, and jobs are submitted to the encoder for compression.
Preview window	The Preview window compares the source media and the proposed target settings. This window also lets you define the section of the source media that the encoder will process, and it lets you place chapter, podcast, and compression markers to support interactivity and encoding.

Standard Window	Function
History window	This window provides easy access to current and completed encoding jobs. Past jobs can be imported back into Compressor for reference or resubmission.
Inspector window	The Inspector window serves as a portal to information and settings. The window's display changes depending on what is selected in the Settings and Batch windows. If a media file is selected, information regarding that file is displayed in the Inspector. If a target or destination is selected, the preset attributes are displayed.
Settings window	This window allows the creation, organization, duplication, and deletion of both settings and destinations. This window can also automatically detect the metadata of QuickTime media and create custom settings based on those parameters.

Batch Window

The Batch window lets you manage your encoding tasks. With a combination of main menus, shortcut menus, and buttons, the Batch window provides access to all the essential components of Compressor.

Compressor displays this window configuration when you open Compressor, or choose File > New Batch From Template.

Select this option to remove the Batch Template Chooser from the default Batch window layout.

TIP You can also set the default display of the Batch window by choosing Compressor > Preferences and setting the For New Batches parameter to the desired choice: Show Template Chooser or Use Blank Template.

When you start with a blank template (empty job with no targets), the Batch window is divided into two sections: an upper section containing the toolbar, and a lower section that contains the individual batches in tabs with any jobs they contain.

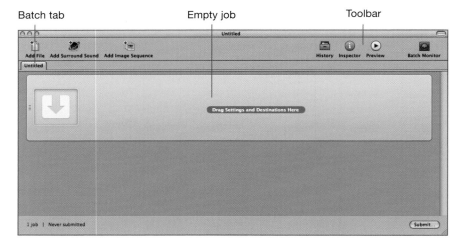

The Batch window toolbar gives you one-click access to the other Compressor windows. If a window is currently visible, click its button to activate it. If the window is not visible, click its button to both open and activate that window.

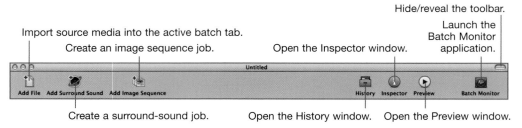

You can customize the toolbar by selecting the Batch window and choosing View > Customize Toolbar.

Use icons in the drop-down window to add buttons to the toolbar.

Drag and drop the tool icons to the desired location on the toolbar.

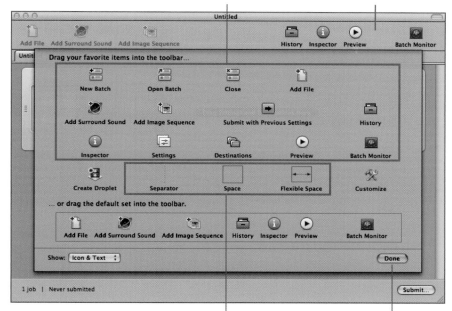

Use Separator, Space, and Flexible Space icons to organize the toolbar.

Click Done when you're finished customizing.

Batch windows let you import source media (called *jobs*) and assign encoding tasks (called *targets*) to each job. Targets are comprised of both a setting and a destination. You can create multiple jobs, each with multiple targets, which together comprise a *batch* that you can submit to encode as one session.

The name of the batch displays in the tab

A job in the Batch tab

Multiple targets assigned to a single job

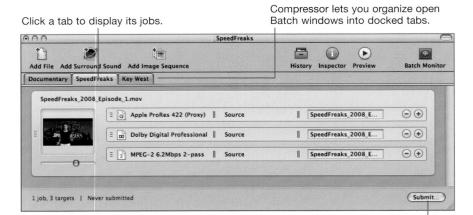

A single target assigned to a job

Displays the current number of jobs and targets in the batch and their submission status

Both jobs together comprise the batch.

Click a tab to display its jobs.

Compressor lets you organize open Batch windows into docked tabs.

The Submit button sends only the jobs of the active batch to the encoder for processing. You can continue working on other open batches and submit them when ready.

Both the toolbar and tabs of the Batch window provide context-specific menus depending on where you Control-click (or right-click).

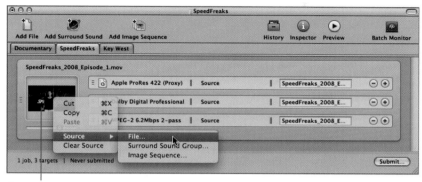

Control-clicking (or right-clicking) a job's thumbnail lets you perform these functions, including importing new source media with the Source > File command.

The Preview Window

The Preview window is divided into three areas: Display controls, Preview screen, and Timeline controls. It offers real-time playback of source material and an output preview of the Filters and Geometry target attributes. Refer to the strategies discussed in Lesson 5, "Test Clip Workflows" for previewing Encoder and Frame Controls settings.

Display controls

Preview screen

Timeline controls

Display Controls and Preview Screen

The Display Control buttons and pop-up menus let you manage how the Preview window presents the native source media and the source media with the currently selected setting (target) applied. The Preview screen plays back the currently selected source media or applied target as a real-time preview.

The Batch Item buttons navigate forward and backward through the currently available media in the Batch window.

The Batch Item pop-up menu provides quick access to the media and targets loaded into the Batch window. It also displays the currently active item in the Preview screen.

The Source/Setting selection buttons control the aspect ratio and frame size of the Preview screen. See the following table for more information.

The Preview scale selection pop-up menu adjusts the size of the Preview window relative to the source media or output file. The menu offers three choices: 100%, 75%, or 50% (see table). The Preview window can correct for pixel aspect ratio by selecting that option. You can set a custom window size by dragging the window's lower-right corner.

The Source/Setting selection buttons can be somewhat confusing when used in tandem with the Preview screen. The following table clarifies how to use these buttons.

You Want To:	Click This Button:
Watch playback of source media	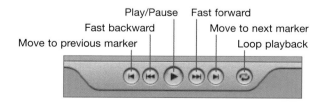 Click the Source button. The choice in the Preview scale selection pop-up menu is relative to the source media. If your source is 720 x 480 pixels, for example, and you choose 50%, the Preview window will scale the playback area to 360 x 240 pixels.
Crop the source media manually	Click the Source button. Note that the red cropping boundaries are available only when the Source button is selected.
Watch a preview relative to the output media—that is, view a particular target in its output dimensions rather than the source's native dimensions	Click the Output button. The choice in the Preview scale selection pop-up menu is relative to the output media. If the output dimension is 320 x 240 pixels, for example, choosing 50% will scale the playback area in the Preview window to 160 x 120 pixels.
View any manual crop settings or crop values that were applied in the Geometry pane of the Inspector	Click the Output button. The cropping boundaries will disappear, and the Source/Output information display will reflect the output frame size and rate.

Timeline Controls

During media playback, the Preview window uses standard transport controls much like those in QuickTime Player or in Final Cut Pro's Viewer and Canvas windows.

Play/Pause
Fast forward
Fast backward
Move to next marker
Move to previous marker
Loop playback

In addition to using the transport controls, you can also scrub the Timeline by dragging the playhead. For more precise control, use the timecode field to the left of the Timeline.

Playhead

Enter the exact frame in the timecode field or click the up and down triangles on either side to move the playhead forward or backward one frame at a time.

You can set In and Out points in the Timeline to define a section of source media bound for encoding.

Click to set an In point at the current position of the playhead.

This area displays the source/ output frame size and rate along with the In to Out duration.

In point   Out point

Click to set an Out point at the current position of the playhead.

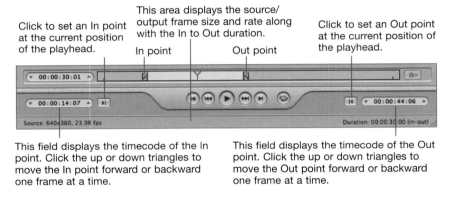

This field displays the timecode of the In point. Click the up or down triangles to move the In point forward or backward one frame at a time.

This field displays the timecode of the Out point. Click the up or down triangles to move the Out point forward or backward one frame at a time.

In tandem with the playhead position, press I or O on the keyboard to set the In and Out points, respectively.

NOTE ▶ If source media has a timecode track, it will be displayed in the timecode field; otherwise, the source media will begin at 00:00:00:00.

The History Window

The History window provides convenient access to recent encoding jobs and targets, allowing you to quickly re-enter them into your Compressor workflow. The History window lists the batches by date.

Click the disclosure triangle to see all the batches for a certain submission date. By default, more recent batches appear at the top of the list.

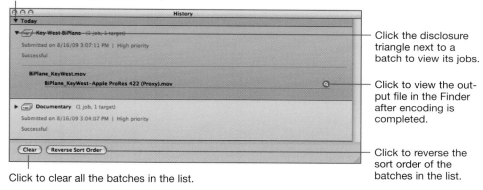

Click the disclosure triangle next to a batch to view its jobs.

Click to view the output file in the Finder after encoding is completed.

Click to reverse the sort order of the batches in the list.

Click to clear all the batches in the list.

You can re-import an entire batch by dragging the entry from the History window into the Batch window.

> **NOTE** ▶ When importing previous batches from the History window, Compressor will create a new "Untitled" batch based on the original source and target settings. You can change or modify the batch as you choose, and then resubmit it. If any source clips have been moved or deleted from their original locations, you will have to manually relink the jobs in the Batch window to the original source media or alternatively import new source media for the job.

The History window also displays the status of currently encoding batches.

Click the disclosure triangle to view all jobs in the batch.

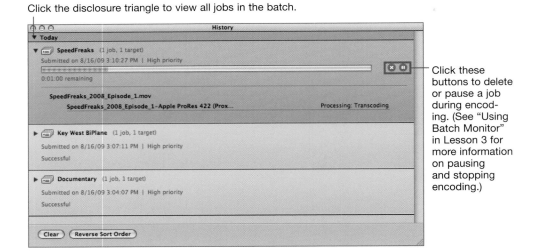

Click these buttons to delete or pause a job during encoding. (See "Using Batch Monitor" in Lesson 3 for more information on pausing and stopping encoding.)

The Inspector Window

The Inspector window is your portal to Compressor's brain, providing access to all the inner workings and parameters that define settings, actions, and destinations. It also displays the most useful information about the imported source media.

For the Inspector to display anything, though, you have to select a job or target in the Batch window or a setting in the Settings window. If nothing is selected, the Inspector window remains empty except for a "Nothing Selected" message.

If source media is selected in the Batch window, the Inspector details the specs of the imported file.

The A/V Attributes tab displays the audio and video parameters of the source media.

See Lesson 9 for details about the Additional Information tab.

See Lesson 4 for more information about the Job Action tab.

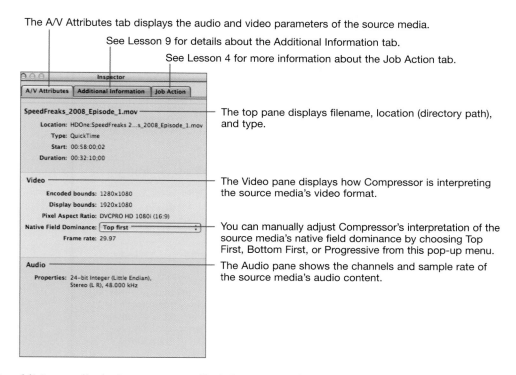

The top pane displays filename, location (directory path), and type.

The Video pane displays how Compressor is interpreting the source media's video format.

You can manually adjust Compressor's interpretation of the source media's native field dominance by choosing Top First, Bottom First, or Progressive from this pop-up menu.

The Audio pane shows the channels and sample rate of the source media's audio content.

In addition to displaying source media information, the Inspector provides detailed access to all the settings and destinations. Depending on which setting you've selected from the Settings window, or which target you've selected from the Batch window, the Inspector will display different interfaces that let you interact with the applicable parameters. The vast majority of custom work you perform in Compressor will employ the Inspector window, and your desired output media type will dictate largely how you modify an item's settings.

These two fields display the Name and Description of the selected preset. The generic "Selected Target" displays when a target is selected from a job in the Batch window.

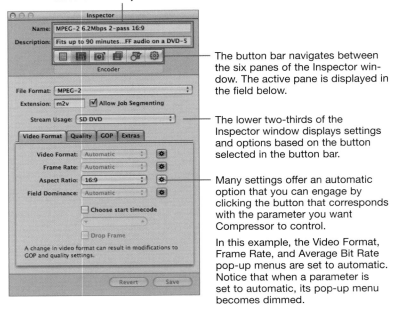

The button bar navigates between the six panes of the Inspector window. The active pane is displayed in the field below.

The lower two-thirds of the Inspector window displays settings and options based on the button selected in the button bar.

Many settings offer an automatic option that you can engage by clicking the button that corresponds with the parameter you want Compressor to control.

In this example, the Video Format, Frame Rate, and Average Bit Rate pop-up menus are set to automatic. Notice that when a parameter is set to automatic, its pop-up menu becomes dimmed.

The Inspector window's appearance when working with settings

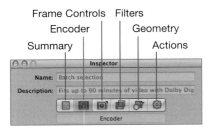

A closer look at the Inspector's button bar

NOTE ▶ See Lesson 4 for more specific information regarding using the Inspector window to modify settings, destinations, and actions..

This field displays the name of the selected output file destination. When creating custom destinations, type the desired name here.

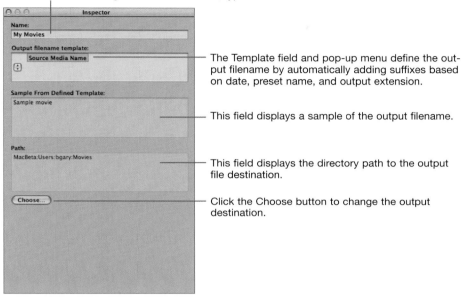

The Template field and pop-up menu define the output filename by automatically adding suffixes based on date, preset name, and output extension.

This field displays a sample of the output filename.

This field displays the directory path to the output file destination.

Click the Choose button to change the output destination.

The Inspector window's appearance when working with destinations

The Settings Window

Compressor encodes for media platforms ranging from Blu-ray Discs and DVDs to Apple TVs and iPhones, from lossless transcodes to audio and video podcasts. Each of those compression targets is governed by a *setting* and is output to a *destination*. The Settings window lets you manage the library of stock Apple settings and destinations that install with Compressor, and also the library of custom settings and destinations that you create yourself.

You access the two sections of the Settings window by selecting the Settings or Destinations tab in the upper-left corner of the window.

Settings Tab

The Settings tab displays two folders containing presets you can apply as targets to jobs in the Batch window. When you install Compressor, all of the stock Apple settings are placed in the Apple folder; presets that you create are saved to the Custom folder.

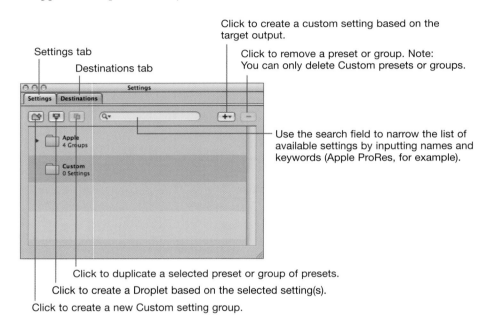

Settings tab

Destinations tab

Click to create a custom setting based on the target output.

Click to remove a preset or group. Note: You can only delete Custom presets or groups.

Use the search field to narrow the list of available settings by inputting names and keywords (Apple ProRes, for example).

Click to duplicate a selected preset or group of presets.

Click to create a Droplet based on the selected setting(s).

Click to create a new Custom setting group.

To view the contents of a folder, click the disclosure triangle to the left of the folder.

Destinations Tab

Each target assigned to a job in the Batch window must have a local or remote destination for the output file. The Destinations tab includes both the default Apple destinations and any custom destinations you define.

Click to duplicate the
selected destination
or group.

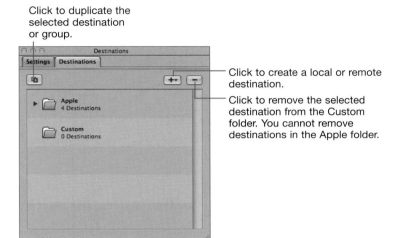

Click to create a local or remote
destination.

Click to remove the selected
destination from the Custom
folder. You cannot remove
destinations in the Apple folder.

To view the contents of a folder, click the disclosure triangle to the left of the folder.

Window Layouts

Compressor's default window layout is called Standard and it appears in two screen
resolutions: 1440 x 900 and 1280 x 800. As a frame of reference, if you are working on
a 15-inch MacBook Pro and choose the Standard 1440 x 900 layout, the Compressor
windows will fill your screen real estate to the edges.

NOTE ▶ The three Batch layouts and the two Standard layouts cannot be deleted.

Compressor also installs with a Batch layout that displays in three screen resolutions:
1440 x 900, 1280 x 800, and 1024 x 768.

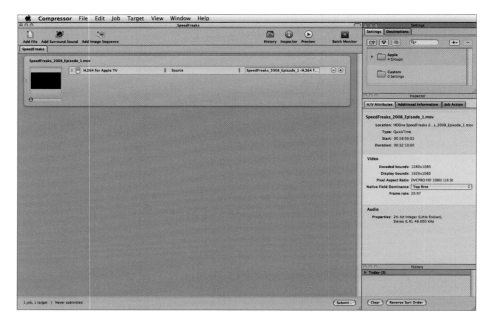

The Batch layouts emphasize an expanded work area suitable for manipulating jobs in the Batch window with easy access to the Inspector window.

To use a predefined window layout, choose Window > Layouts and select the desired orientation and resolution.

In addition to the layouts that install with Compressor, you can create custom layouts and save them for future use. For example, you may find that a layout including Batch, Preview, and Settings windows works best with batches that require no setting customization.

TIP You can adjust multiple windows simultaneously by placing your cursor between two or more windows and dragging the group.

Once you have designed a window arrangement that suits your needs, choose Window > Save Layout. Name the layout and click Save.

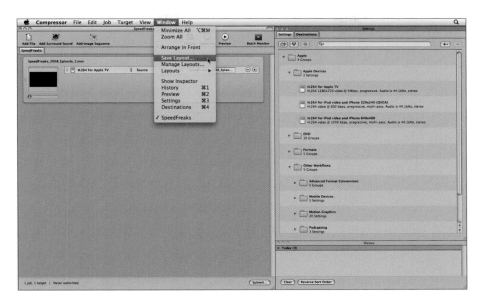

Choose Window > Manage Layouts to add or delete custom window arrangements.

You can arrange Compressor's windows with this drop-down window open.
Click the Add (+) button to add a new layout. Name it and click Done.

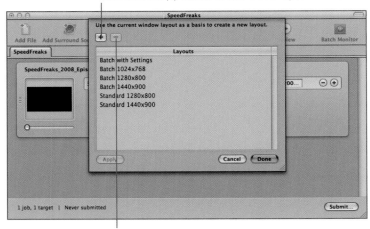

Click to remove any selected layouts from the list.

To evaluate your understanding of the concepts covered in this lesson and to prepare
for the Apple Pro Certification Exam, download the online quiz at www.peachpit.com/
apts.compressor.

2

Core Concepts

- Understand batch templates
- Publish to Blu-ray Disc
- Publish to MobileMe
- Integrate batch templates with manual workflows

Lesson 2
Publishing with Batch Templates

Batch templates create a simplified, streamlined pathway through Compressor that allows you to choose the direction of the encoding process based on the final published media and not on the encoded files. When you're first learning how to use Compressor, batch templates provide a launchpad for content encoding that teaches you about digital delivery while simultaneously producing final media.

Batch templates include all of the necessary encoding settings for the most common forms of digital distribution used during post-production: DVDs, Blu-ray Discs, media for Apple devices (iPhones, iPods, and Apple TVs), and movies published to the Web via YouTube and MobileMe.

As a result, you don't need an extensive knowledge of codecs and formats to produce high-quality media using Compressor. In a few easy steps, Compressor can create the final product, and you can focus on creating and distributing your content.

Batch templates are self-contained workflows through Compressor and don't require any other application. For example, if you choose the DVD template, Compressor will not only create the files needed to make the DVD, but it will author and burn the final disc, based on its analysis of the source movie and the template's parameters.

Working with batch templates comprises four basic steps:

1   Choose a batch template.

2   Import a source media file.

3   Customize the job action.

4   Submit the batch for processing.

Each batch template employs the same basic methodology when producing the encoded media for final output. The templates differ, though, in the implementation of their post-encoding tasks, called *job actions*. The Compressor Help documents describe each of the standard Apple batch templates and their general use. This lesson will demonstrate two practical applications of batch templates.

In addition to the batch templates that install with Compressor, you can create custom templates that will appear with the default ones (see Lesson 4, "Working with Actions").

> **TIP** ▶ The Easy Export option found in both Final Cut Pro and Motion utilizes Compressor's core batch templates. This interface lets you choose the same encoding targets and job actions described in this lesson. Refer to the Final Cut Pro and Motion Help documents for more information on Easy Export via the File > Share menu option.

Publishing to Blu-ray Disc

The Create Blu-ray batch template enables the production of Blu-ray-compatible audio and video files and the burning of a Blu-ray-compatible disc.

> **NOTE** ▶ Blu-ray Disc burning (BD and AVCHD) using the batch templates is only supported on computers when Final Cut Studio is installed.

Choosing a Batch Template

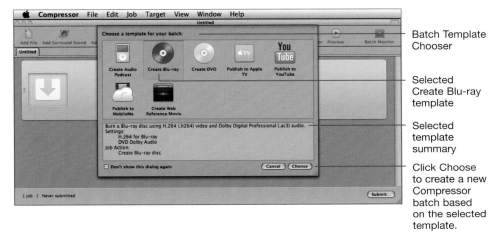

Batch Template Chooser

Selected Create Blu-ray template

Selected template summary

Click Choose to create a new Compressor batch based on the selected template.

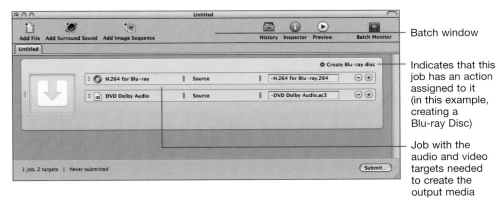

Batch window

Indicates that this job has an action assigned to it (in this example, creating a Blu-ray Disc)

Job with the audio and video targets needed to create the output media

Importing Source Media

After selecting the template, define the source media by dragging a QuickTime-compatible file from the Finder onto the job in the Batch window. In this example, an episode of the high-definition television series SpeedFreaks (www.speedfreaks.tv) will be used to create the Blu-ray Disc.

Drag the QuickTime source file onto
the job in the Batch window.

Finder window with QuickTime-
compatible source media

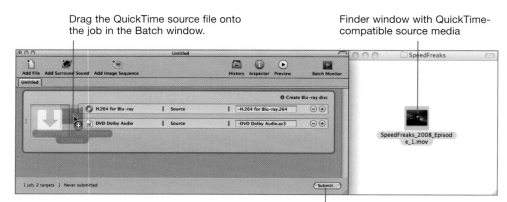

Click Submit to send the batch to the encoder.

Refer to Lesson 3 for more information on importing source media into Compressor.

NOTE ▶ Each batch template has only a single job and can therefore process only
a single piece of source media. If you drag multiple files onto a batch template,
Compressor will use only one as the source media.

Select the job in the Batch window to open it in the Inspector
window.

Note: Selecting a target instead of the job will load encoding
parameters into the Inspector. If you inadvertently select a
target, just click directly on the job to reopen it in the Inspector.

Click the Job Action tab
to view the settings.

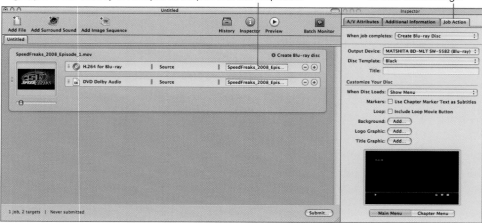

TIP ▶ Compressor assigns an "H.264 for Blu-ray" target for the video and a DVD Dolby Audio target for the audio stream because Blu-ray authoring requires that the audio and video elements be separated into individual assets called Elementary Streams.

Customizing the Job Action

Some batch templates, such as the Blu-ray Disc template, do not *need* to be customized, but making them unique to your particular project adds a higher level of production value to your published disc. For example, placing a background image on the menus adds a distinctive touch to a stock template.

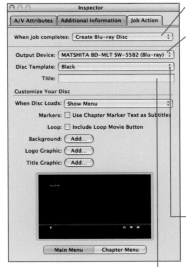

Input a custom title that will appear on both menus.

This menu displays the batch template's default action. You can change the action with this pop-up menu (see Lesson 4).

All available media burners will appear in this pop-up menu. See the following table for more information on BD and AVCHD discs.

In this example, both an external, third-party Blu-ray burner and an internal SuperDrive (DVD) are available.

Note: Choose the Hard Drive option to create a Blu-ray Disc image that you can use to later burn optical media using Disk Utility or Roxio's Toast (www.roxio.com).

Choose the disc template that will govern the Main and Chapter menus.

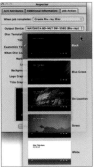

Some menus include motion elements; others are static. Choose the theme that best suits your source media.

The following table illustrates the differences between the two types of burned media that the Create Blu-ray Disc Job Action can produce.

Format	BD	AVCHD
Media Type	Blu-ray Disc	DVD-5 and DVD-9
Capacity	25 GB (50 GB for dual layer discs)	4.7 GB and 8.5 GB
Laser Type	Blue	Red
Max Bit Rate	35 Mbps	17 Mbps
Subtitles	Supported	Not supported
Menu Features	Full template support	Basic template support

Support for burned BD or AVCHD media varies from player to player. Refer to your hardware manufacturer's documentation or website for compatibility specifications.

NOTE ▶ You cannot natively play discs that contain either form of Blu-ray Disc content (BD or AVCHD) on a Mac computer.

Define whether the movie or the main menu plays first when disc playback starts.

Note: If you choose Play Movie, the main menu will display after the movie finishes.

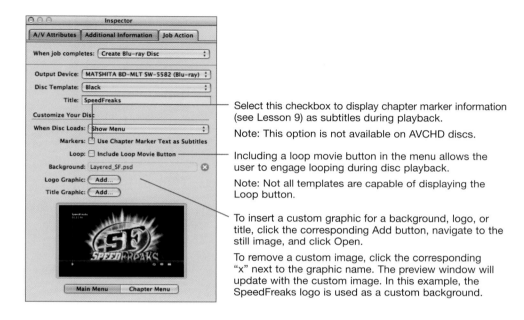

Select this checkbox to display chapter marker information (see Lesson 9) as subtitles during playback.

Note: This option is not available on AVCHD discs.

Including a loop movie button in the menu allows the user to engage looping during disc playback.

Note: Not all templates are capable of displaying the Loop button.

To insert a custom graphic for a background, logo, or title, click the corresponding Add button, navigate to the still image, and click Open.

To remove a custom image, click the corresponding "x" next to the graphic name. The preview window will update with the custom image. In this example, the SpeedFreaks logo is used as a custom background.

> **TIP** The Create DVD batch template has a reduced set of job action options compared to the Create Blu-ray template. Mastering the previously described procedure will fully prepare you to publish DVDs, as well as BD and AVCHD media, when using the batch template workflow.

Submitting the Batch

After customizing the job action, the batch is ready for processing. In the Batch window, click Submit to send the batch to the encoder.

Enter a name for the batch and click Submit in this drop-down window.

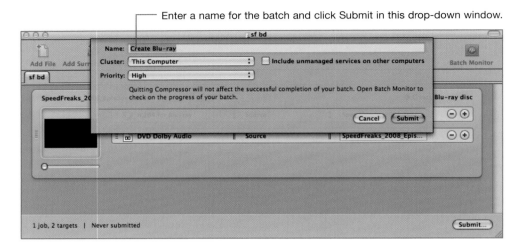

You can oversee the encoding process in the History window (see Lesson 1) or Batch Monitor (see Lesson 4).

After the assets for the Create Blu-ray batch template are finished encoding, the Create Disc application will open and request the insertion of blank optical media.

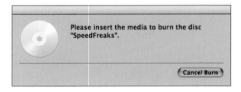

Based on your choice in the Output Device pop-up menu, insert a blank Blu-ray Disc or DVD into your optical drive.

> NOTE ▶ Canceling the batch at this point will stop the burn process, but the encoded media will remain in the output location as defined by the batch template.

You can continue to monitor progress in the History window or Batch Monitor. When the batch is completed, the optical drive will eject the finished media and Create Disc will display this dialog:

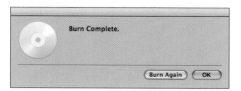

Clicking Burn Again creates another disc without re-encoding the source media. Click OK when you are finished burning discs.

> **NOTE ▶** If you end the session by clicking OK but later want to create additional discs, you will need to resubmit the batch and reprocess the job from the beginning.

Publishing to MobileMe

MobileMe galleries provide a convenient way to globally distribute your content via the Internet. The "Publish to MobileMe" batch template not only outputs the proper media, but it also uploads the movies to the online service and creates a Web Gallery where your audience can view and download the content.

Using this batch template requires a MobileMe account and Internet access for uploading, managing, and viewing the online galleries.

> **TIP▶** Since the batch template workflow is a simplified path through Compressor, many of the steps outlined in this section are similar to those previously described in the "Publishing to Blu-ray Disc" section. Learn the differences in each of the templates' encoding settings (targets) and job actions to understand which file formats serve each delivery platform. For example, output media appropriate for a DVD is different from media that is suitable for an iPhone. The batch templates are not only an easy way to publish content within Final Cut Studio, they can also instruct you in core compression concepts.

Choosing a Batch Template

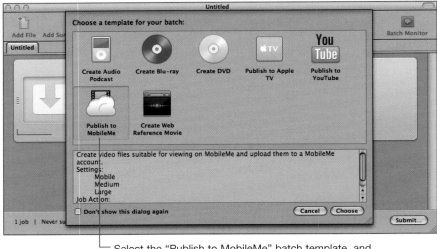

Select the "Publish to MobileMe" batch template, and then click Choose.

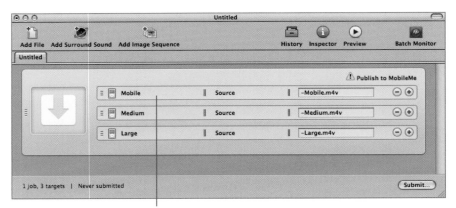

The job fills with all possible encoding settings (targets) for MobileMe delivery.

By default, the "Publish to MobileMe" template creates three output-encoding settings for the job. Each one will produce a media file that targets a specific audience: Mobile targets iPhone, Medium targets iPod, and Large targets Apple TV. You use the batch template to either create all three file formats and let your audience choose a desired format, or you could reduce the number of output files (and available viewing options) by selecting one or two targets to remove and pressing Delete. However, at least one of the delivery targets must remain for a valid "Publish to MobileMe" batch template.

TIP Each of the targets are based on settings found in the Apple Devices folder of the Settings window.

Importing Source Media

Drag the QuickTime source file from the Finder onto the job in the Batch window.

Refer to Lesson 3 for more information on importing source media.

Customizing the Job Action

Although many batch templates do not require user customization, other templates, such as "Publish to MobileMe," require user input before they can process.

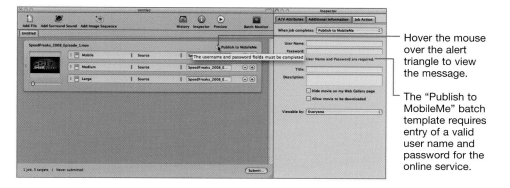

Hover the mouse over the alert triangle to view the message.

The "Publish to MobileMe" batch template requires entry of a valid user name and password for the online service.

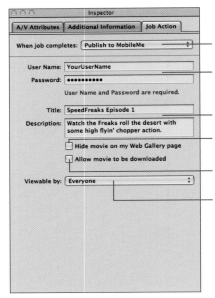

You can change the batch template's default action with this pop-up menu (see Lesson 4).

Enter your MobileMe user name and password in these fields.

Enter a Title and Description to appear on the movie's webpage.

Selecting this checkbox will hide links to the movie's page on your existing MobileMe gallery pages.

Selecting this checkbox allows movie downloading and/or streaming from the site.

This pop-up menu defines audience permissions for viewing movies.

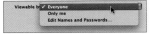

Choose Everyone to allow open access to the movies via the Internet.

Choose "Only me" to restrict access to the movie to anyone with your MobileMe user name and password.

Choose "Edit Names and Passwords" to open the following dialog:

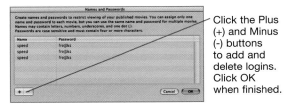

Click the Plus (+) and Minus (-) buttons to add and delete logins. Click OK when finished.

You can only define a single login for each MobileMe batch template. If you have multiple jobs in the batch, use the same login for each entry.

Submitting the Batch

After customizing the job action, the batch is ready for processing. In the Batch window, click Submit to send the batch to the encoder.

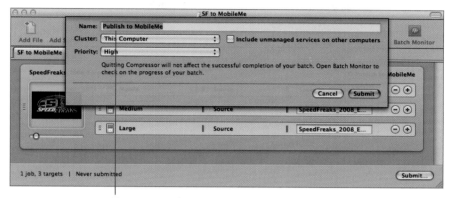

Enter a name for the batch, and then click Submit.

You can oversee the encoding process in the History window (see Lesson 1) or Batch Monitor (see Lesson 4). After the MobileMe movies are encoded, Compressor will upload them to the online service and create a Web Gallery. When the batch successfully completes, log in to your MobileMe account with Safari and click the Gallery button.

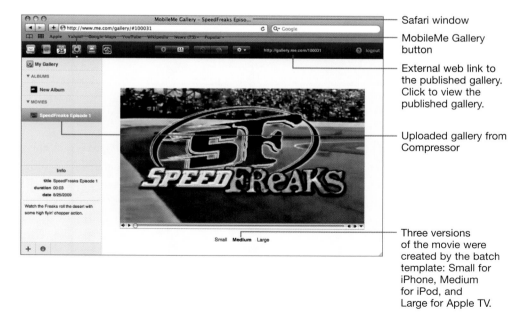

Safari window

MobileMe Gallery button

External web link to the published gallery. Click to view the published gallery.

Uploaded gallery from Compressor

Three versions of the movie were created by the batch template: Small for iPhone, Medium for iPod, and Large for Apple TV.

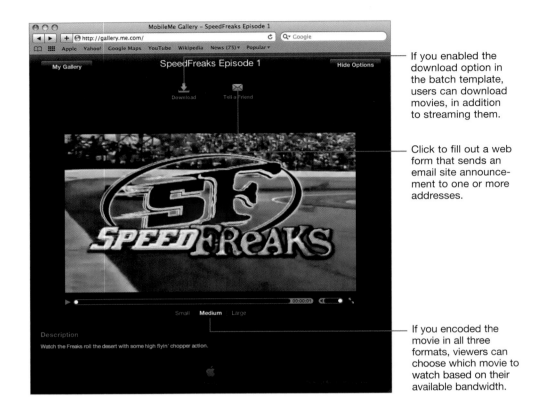

If you enabled the download option in the batch template, users can download movies, in addition to streaming them.

Click to fill out a web form that sends an email site announcement to one or more addresses.

If you encoded the movie in all three formats, viewers can choose which movie to watch based on their available bandwidth.

Integrating Batch Templates with Manual Workflows

In addition to the streamlined batch templates, Compressor offers an alternative path through the application. This hands-on workflow allows the selection and customization of the encoding parameters, thereby defining exactly the type of output media your delivery specification requires. Lessons 3 and 4 cover this core Compressor workflow in detail.

Batch templates provide simple solutions for some common delivery platforms, but even after you've "graduated" from using batch templates exclusively and transitioned to Compressor's manual workflows, batch templates still provide a fast and efficient method of producing content in Final Cut Studio.

As your skills with both Compressor and compression increase, you'll undoubtedly find you employ a mixture of templates, Droplets (see Lesson 4), and manual workflows depending on the project at hand. Batch templates are not only quick and easy, they are often the best path for the job.

To evaluate your understanding of the concepts covered in this lesson and to prepare for the Apple Pro Certification Exam, download the online quiz at www.peachpit.com/apts.compressor.

3

Core Concepts

Export a QuickTime movie from Final Cut Pro

Import QuickTime media to Compressor

Export files from Soundtrack Pro

Submit a batch (source media) for encoding

Check status and manage the encoding process with Batch Monitor

Lesson 3
Batch Encoding

Compressor not only delivers media from Final Cut Studio to the rest of the world, it's also the post-production workhorse for transcoding media files from one format to another. While it can, for example, transform a Final Cut Pro sequence into H.264 and Dolby Digital Professional assets that are appropriate for a Blu-ray Disc, it can also use the Apple ProRes production codecs to transcode HD camera footage into formats suited to workflows inside Final Cut Studio.

The true power of Compressor is unleashed when you manage the flow of audio and video sources through its Batch window. Although importing source media and applying targets to jobs in the Batch window are among the core functions of the Compressor workflow, the ability to queue up disparate encoding jobs, called a *batch,* and monitor their progress during processing is what makes Compressor the centerpiece of your entire digital distribution pipeline.

Using the Core Compressor Workflow

In the context of using batch templates, the previous lesson described a basic Compressor workflow: Choose where you want to deliver content, customize any of the actions, and finally submit the batch for encoding.

The core Compressor workflow, more suitable for intermediate and advanced use, entails three basic steps:

1   Import source media into a job in the Batch window.

2   Assign a target to the job (includes encoder, destination, and output filename).

   Repeat steps 1 and 2 for as many source and output media files that your particular project requires.

3   Submit the batch for processing.

The primary difference between the batch template workflow and the core Compressor workflow is production focus. Meaning, in the batch template workflow you only need to know what you want to produce, such as a Blu-ray Disc or a YouTube-ready movie. In the core Compressor workflow, you need to know the *type* of media files you want to produce. This manual path through Compressor allows the advanced user with extensive compression experience to manipulate and tweak the encoding settings for specific results.

The next two lessons outline the core Compressor workflow. This lesson details the importing and managing of media, or jobs, within Compressor. Lesson 4 will examine settings, targets, and actions.

Exporting from Final Cut Pro

You can export Final Cut Pro sequences to Compressor in one of three ways: by exporting a QuickTime movie, by using the Share command, or by using the Send To command.

Exporting a QuickTime Movie

This method renders a final movie of the sequence as either a self-contained or reference QuickTime movie that can be imported directly into Compressor.

With a sequence loaded in the Timeline, make the Timeline the active window.

NOTE ▶ To export the entire sequence, remove any In or Out points from the Timeline; otherwise Final Cut Pro will export only the portion of the sequence between the user-defined In and Out points.

Choose File >
Export > QuickTime
Movie, or press
Command-E.

Define the output file in the Save dialog that opens.

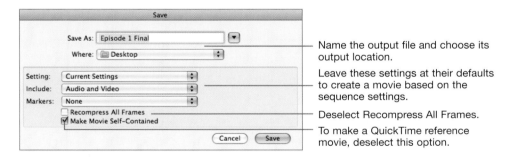

Name the output file and choose its output location.

Leave these settings at their defaults to create a movie based on the sequence settings.

Deselect Recompress All Frames.

To make a QuickTime reference movie, deselect this option.

NOTE ▶ QuickTime reference movies, although significantly smaller in file size than self-contained movies, will play properly only on the systems on which they were created because the movie is actually referencing local media and render files. Create self-contained movies when you need to move the exported file to another system.

Refer to the section "Importing QuickTime Media" in this lesson for methods on using exported Final Cut Pro files within Compressor.

Using the Share Command

Final Cut Pro's Share command provides output options similar to Compressor's batch templates.

With a sequence loaded in the Timeline, select the Timeline window to make it the active window, and choose File > Share.

> **NOTE** ▶ You can export files from Motion to Compressor using the same File > Share command.

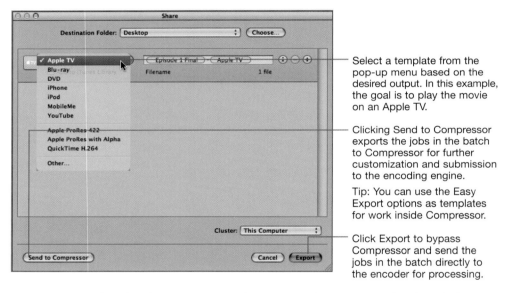

Select a template from the pop-up menu based on the desired output. In this example, the goal is to play the movie on an Apple TV.

Clicking Send to Compressor exports the jobs in the batch to Compressor for further customization and submission to the encoding engine.

Tip: You can use the Easy Export options as templates for work inside Compressor.

Click Export to bypass Compressor and send the jobs in the batch directly to the encoder for processing.

If you choose to send the batch, Compressor will open, populate an empty batch with the sequence, and apply any targets and actions you defined in Final Cut Pro's Share window.

Using the Send To Command

Final Cut Pro's Send To Compressor command will export a sequence directly to Compressor without the need to render or output any sequence media before encoding. The rendering (including effects, composites, transitions, and so on) will occur during the encoding process.

NOTE ► Rendered elements (if any) will appear only in the final output media from Compressor. This process will not create sequence render files that you can use when editing in Final Cut Pro.

With a sequence opened in the Timeline, make the Timeline window active, and choose File > Send To > Compressor.

If it's not already open, Compressor will open and populate an empty batch with the sequence. If Compressor is currently running and you already have an active batch, a new Batch window will be created and docked as a tab. A new Batch window is also created if you send additional sequences from Final Cut Pro during the same Compressor session.

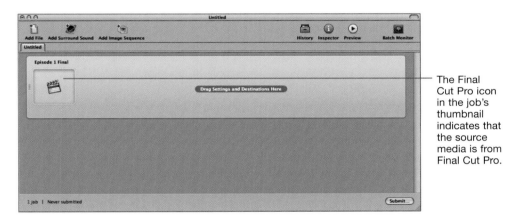

The Final Cut Pro icon in the job's thumbnail indicates that the source media is from Final Cut Pro.

See Lesson 4 to learn techniques for assigning targets, destinations, and actions to sequences imported from Final Cut Pro.

TIP In addition to sending sequences from the Final Cut Pro Timeline window using File menu commands, you can Control-click (or right-click) a sequence in the Browser window and access the same set of commands in the Export and Send To shortcut menus.

Interaction Between Final Cut Pro and Compressor

When sending sequences from Final Cut Pro to Compressor using the Send To command, you will want to consider some benefits and compromises to the workflow.

When sending directly from Final Cut Pro to Compressor, the native frames from the sequence are sent; that is, they are not first rendered into the sequence settings. This not only saves drive space, but it also passes the highest quality media to Compressor for encoding.

Additionally, you can send sequences to Compressor and continue working inside Final Cut Pro. You can even continue editing the sequence you just sent, with a few limitations:

►   Because Final Cut Pro is performing all sequence-based renders for Compressor in the background, Final Cut Pro performance may degrade when sending sequences with extensive compositing, effects, or mixed media. The more powerful your Mac, the better the overall performance will be.

►   If a Final Cut Pro sequence is currently encoding in Compressor, you can send additional sequences to Compressor, but you will not be able to access them in the Preview window or begin processing them until the previous job is completed. This alert message will appear in the Preview window:

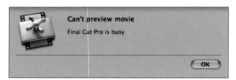

►   If you reopen a batch for resubmission from the History window and it contains a job that originated as a Final Cut Pro sequence, Compressor will need to open Final Cut Pro to access the source media. Therefore, the Final Cut Pro project and its associated assets will need to reside on the same system as the Compressor batch you are attempting to resubmit.

►   If you are submitting batches with Final Cut Pro sequences to a cluster (see Lesson 12), Final Cut Pro will have to be installed on all the nodes *and* those nodes will need read access to all the source media referenced in the sequence.

Importing QuickTime Media

Compressor can import any media file for which QuickTime has an appropriate playback codec. If QuickTime Player can open a file, Compressor can import it.

NOTE ▶ Compressor cannot import any media containing Digital Rights Management (DRM) or copy-protection, such as content purchased from the iTunes Store.

You can import source media into Compressor using one of the three following methods:

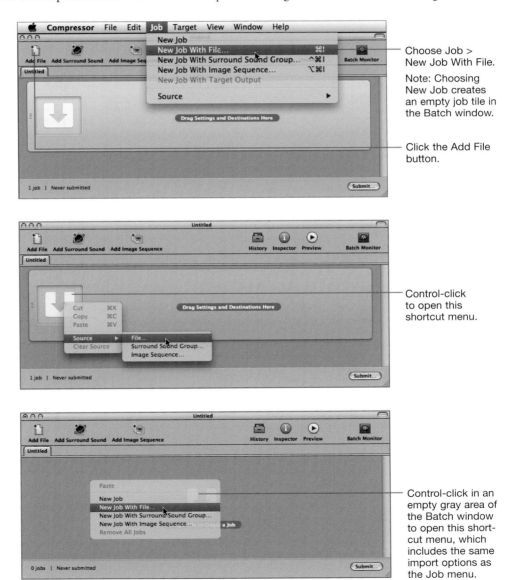

Choose Job > New Job With File.

Note: Choosing New Job creates an empty job tile in the Batch window.

Click the Add File button.

Control-click to open this shortcut menu.

Control-click in an empty gray area of the Batch window to open this short-cut menu, which includes the same import options as the Job menu.

Any of these methods will display an Open dialog in which you can navigate to your source media, select it, and then click Open.

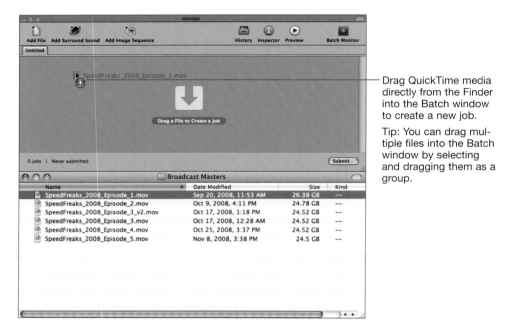

Drag QuickTime media directly from the Finder into the Batch window to create a new job.

Tip: You can drag multiple files into the Batch window by selecting and dragging them as a group.

If you have multiple Batch windows docked as tabs when using any of these methods, make sure you select the desired Batch tab before importing source media. You can also create a new Batch window for the imported QuickTime media by choosing File > New Batch.

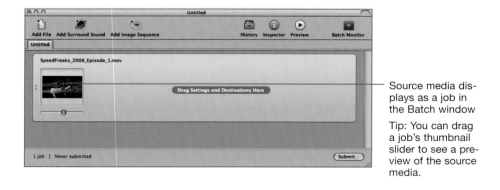

Source media displays as a job in the Batch window

Tip: You can drag a job's thumbnail slider to see a preview of the source media.

TIP ▶ You can import Motion project files directly into Compressor and they will be treated as QuickTime source media files.

Exporting from Soundtrack Pro

All of the Compressor encoding options available to Soundtrack Pro are contained within Soundtrack Pro's export function.

Starting with a completed multi-track project in Soundtrack Pro, choose File > Export.

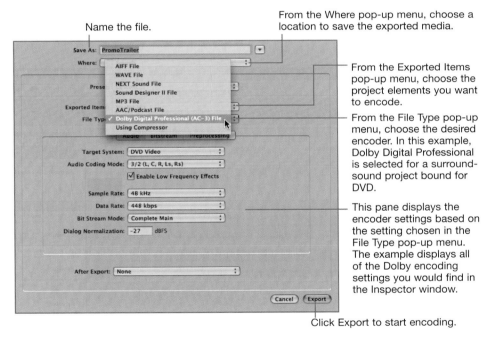

Name the file.

From the Where pop-up menu, choose a location to save the exported media.

From the Exported Items pop-up menu, choose the project elements you want to encode.

From the File Type pop-up menu, choose the desired encoder. In this example, Dolby Digital Professional is selected for a surround-sound project bound for DVD.

This pane displays the encoder settings based on the setting chosen in the File Type pop-up menu. The example displays all of the Dolby encoding settings you would find in the Inspector window.

Click Export to start encoding.

Neither Compressor nor Batch Monitor will launch upon export; the processing occurs within Soundtrack Pro.

This Soundtrack Pro window displays during encoding.

TIP If you've been working with video in Soundtrack Pro, choose Using Compressor from the File Type pop-up menu to either pass the video through the export process or to choose one of the Compressor settings to transcode the video.

Batch Encoding

A batch comprises individual pieces of source media (a job). Any given batch can contain as many jobs as you require. Targets control the encoding process and comprise a setting, a destination, and an output filename. Each job can include multiple targets.

After a batch is saved, its name appears in the tab.

Currently selected job in the Batch window

Job with multiple targets

Sequence exported directly from Final Cut Pro

When a batch is ready for processing, click Submit to send its jobs to the encoder.

The Batch window

Managing and Maximizing Batches

Compressor offers almost unlimited ways to create batches to address your encoding needs. Compressor's versatility is especially useful when the overall estimated encoding time for a series of jobs spans several hours (or days). Instead of submitting and monitoring each job individually, you can batch-organize the sessions and let Compressor perform the laborious task of monitoring each job in the series. Furthermore, a series of jobs and targets in a batch is, in essence, a template for your encoding work. That is, you can save a batch and reuse it by replacing only the source media.

Jobs and targets are the building blocks of batches. You can combine and manipulate them in the Batch window to create more efficient encoding workflows.

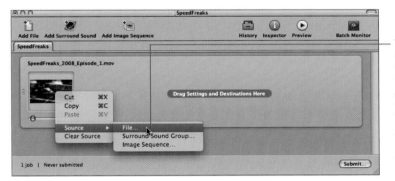

To replace one job's source media with different media, Control-click the job's poster frame, and from the shortcut menu, choose Source > File. In the window that appears, navigate to the new media and click Open.

Click the Minus (-) button to remove a target.

Click the Plus (+) button to add an empty target.

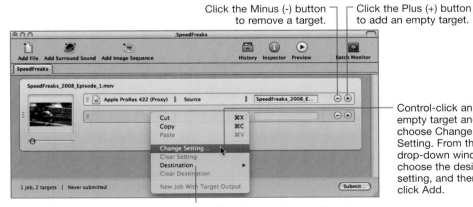

Control-click an empty target and choose Change Setting. From the drop-down window, choose the desired setting, and then click Add.

To add or change the target's output location, choose a destination from the list in the submenu.

Compressor lets you work on jobs and targets individually or as groups. For example, if you have 50 jobs to encode as Apple ProRes 422 (Proxy), make the Batch window active, choose Edit > Select All, and then choose Target > New Target With Setting. From the drop-down window, choose the desired setting and then click Add. The same target will be applied to every job in the batch—a real timesaver.

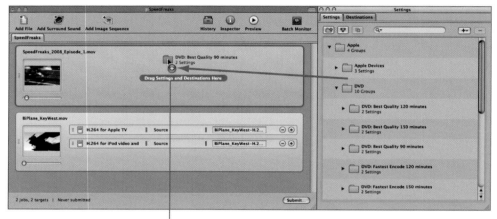

To apply all of a group's settings as separate targets, drag a group (folder) from the Settings window to a job in the Batch window.

Note: You are not limited to groups that just contain settings; you can drag groups that contain other groups as well.

TIP You can create a custom group (folder) that contains all the settings for a particular project or an individual client. Then, you just have to drag the group onto a job to apply all the targets at once, including all the necessary custom settings.

Copying and Pasting Jobs and Targets

In Compressor, you can manage and recycle your work using convenient cut-and-paste methods. Encoding can encompass many repetitive tasks, so copying a target from one job to another within the Batch window is a great timesaving technique.

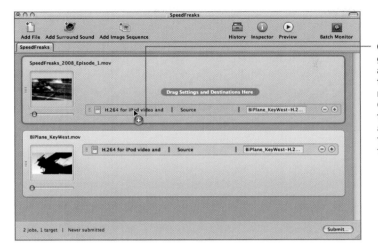

Option-drag a target from one job to another to copy the target. You can copy multiple targets by Command-clicking the desired targets and Option-dragging them as a group to the new job.

To move multiple targets from one job to another, as in this example, Command-click the targets in the bottom job to select them, and then drag them to the top job.

The job window resizes dynamically to accommodate additional targets.

The standard cut, copy, and paste commands in the Edit menu (and their keyboard shortcuts) work with both jobs and targets, so you can cut or copy a target from one job and paste it onto another.

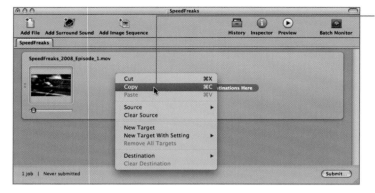

Control-click a job or a specific target, and from the shortcut menu, choose Copy. Continuing with this example, you could paste multiple instances of the same job in the batch by choosing Paste from the short-cut menu (or pressing Command-V). This technique can be use-ful when lining up test encodes. (See Lesson 5 for more information on test clip workflows.)

Creating and Saving Batches

Although Compressor opens with either a template or a single empty batch in the Batch window, you can create as many batches as you need by opening new batches as tabs in the current Batch window. To create a new batch, choose File > New Batch.

Compressor also lets you save batches for use with later encoding jobs, or to more efficiently organize current jobs. To save a batch, make sure the Batch window is active, then choose File > Save. In the drop-down window, name the batch, navigate to the desired save location, and click Save. The batch name will appear in the current tab in the Batch window.

Each batch has its own tab in the Batch window. Click a tab to display the jobs contained in that batch.

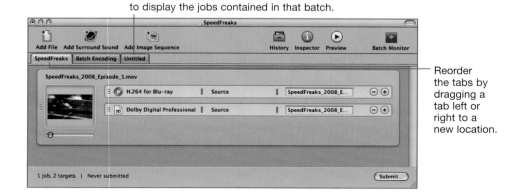

Reorder the tabs by dragging a tab left or right to a new location.

To close a batch tab, select it and choose File > Close Tab.

Tear off a tab by dragging it from its original Batch window. This creates a new
Batch window that contains the jobs from that tab. You can also Control-click a tab
and choose Tear Off Tab from the shortcut menu. To redock a Batch window, drag
its tab onto the tab bar of another Batch window and release the mouse button
when the light blue bounding box appears around the target window's tab bar.

TIP ▸ In Compressor, you can copy, cut, and paste both jobs and targets between
all open batches. So, you can cut a job and its targets from one batch, click the tab of
another batch, and paste the job and all its targets into that batch. This is useful, for
example, when three of the four jobs in a batch are ready for encoding. You can cut
and paste the job that is not yet ready into another batch and then submit the batch
with the three jobs that are ready for processing.

Troubleshooting Batches

When at least one target is applied to all jobs in a batch, you can submit the batch for processing by clicking Submit. If no targets have been applied, Compressor displays an alert
when you click Submit:

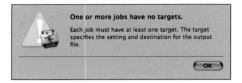

To correct the error, add at least one target to every job in the batch and click Submit.

Batches rely on relative paths to the source media and to the Final Cut Pro sequences or Motion projects they contain. Therefore, if any source media is moved from the location it occupied when the batch was created, Compressor will no longer be able to locate the file and will display an alert.

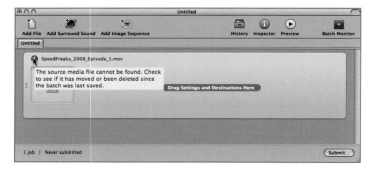

A red alert will appear above the source media poster frame if there is a problem locating source media. Place your pointer over the alert to view the alert details.

To correct a missing media error, Control-click the job's poster frame and choose Source > File from the shortcut menu. In the Open window, navigate to the media's new location and click Open. You can also drag the media directly from the Finder onto the job's poster frame, and Compressor will automatically update the location.

Compressor will also alert you when it encounters a job with the same output filename as a file currently in the target destination.

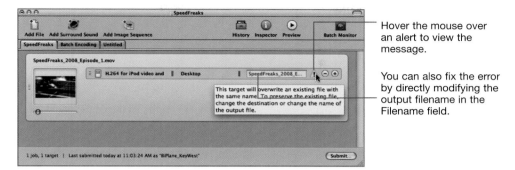

Hover the mouse over an alert to view the message.

You can also fix the error by directly modifying the output filename in the Filename field.

Fix the error by selecting a new destination. Control-click the target and choose a new location from the Destination menu.

NOTE ▶ It's important to understand that this alert will not stop Compressor from encoding the job. If you click Submit without changing the output filename or destination, Compressor will output the file and overwrite the existing file to eliminate the conflict.

Compressor will also display an alert message if two targets within the batch could export files with identical filenames.

Creating Custom Batch Templates

You can streamline routine encoding sessions by creating a batch template from common encoding scenarios. For example, if you consistently encode the same types of media during the early phases of post-production—such as when creating iPod/iPhone screeners and proxy movies—you can, instead, create a batch template and save the time you would spend configuring those jobs manually for every single use.

When you create a new batch, it will open with an empty job by default. Saving the job will display its name in the Batch tab.

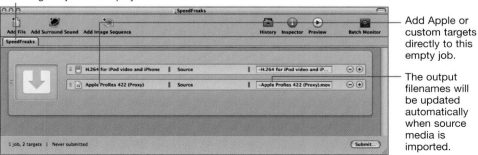

Add Apple or custom targets directly to this empty job.

The output filenames will be updated automatically when source media is imported.

You can define as many targets as you need to fulfill your encoding workflow.

Save the custom batch template by choosing File > Save as Template.

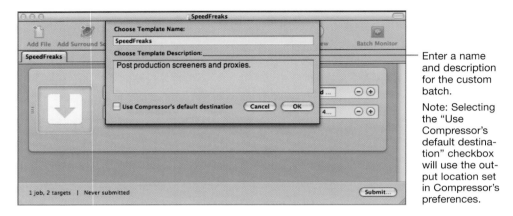

Enter a name and description for the custom batch.

Note: Selecting the "Use Compressor's default destination" checkbox will use the output location set in Compressor's preferences.

To use any of the custom or default batch templates, choose File > New Batch from Template.

Click the custom batch template to select it.

Your custom description appears below, along with a list of included targets.

Click Choose to create a new batch based on the template.

Refer to Lesson 2 for more information on using batch templates as a complete Compressor workflow.

> **TIP** ▶ To remove custom batch templates, delete them at the Finder level: ~/Library/ Application Support/Compressor/Templates/. Delete any unwanted templates from that folder and they will no longer appear in the Batch Template Chooser.

Additionally, any batch you've saved can be used as a template for encoding work inside Compressor.

Finder icon of a saved Compressor batch.

To reuse a saved batch, double-click it in the Finder, or choose File > Open in Compressor and navigate to the saved file. Next, replace the source media with new media. You can submit the batch "as is" or make any adjustments to the targets, and then submit the batch for encoding.

> **TIP** ▶ You can create a batch with a single job or a series of empty jobs that have as few or as many targets as your workflow requires, and then save the batch as a starting point for future Compressor sessions.

Chaining Jobs

Compressor lets you control and refine the encoding process by setting up a series of two or more jobs that use output from a preceding job as their source media. This is known as *job chaining*.

For example, an H.264 encoding job with multi-pass engaged could require three or four passes over the media. If any Frame Controls (see Lesson 6) are enabled, they will process with each pass. Depending on the settings, this situation can lengthen the encoding time considerably. So, instead of encoding the Frame Controls during each pass, you can use a job chain to process them just once and then pass the output of that job to the H.264 job.

> **TIP** ▸ The Apple ProRes 422 (HQ) settings are very good for encoding the interme-
> diate movies that pass between jobs in the chain because they retain picture fidelity and
> are flexible in terms of frame size and frame rate. Apple ProRes 422 (HQ) employs
> a high-quality, 10-bit encoder in a 4:2:2 colorspace. If your processing requires a full
> 4:4:4 colorspace, you can use Apple ProRes 4444.

To create a job chain, import source media, apply a target, and make any necessary changes to the settings. In the following example, an HD clip is being downconverted to a 640 x 360 resolution using Frame Controls. An Apple ProRes 422 (HQ) setting was used as the intermediate codec. You'll find both progressive and interlaced output versions in the Settings window by following this path: Apple > Other Workflows > Advanced Format Conversions > Apple Codecs.

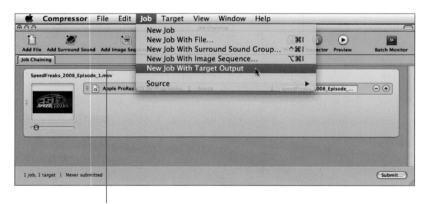

Select the target to which you want to chain the output, and then choose Job > New Job With Target Output.

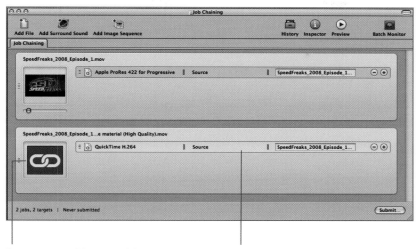

Compressor adds a new job to the batch and displays the chain symbol as the poster frame to indicate that the job requires source media produced by a previous job in the batch. The input filename at the top of the job window also reflects the incoming media.

You can add as many targets as necessary to the chained job. The job will start processing once the previous job passes the new source media to it.

In this example, the 640 x 360 Apple ProRes 422 (HQ) movie output from the first job passes to the next job in the chain where an H.264 encoder is applied. Since the previous job already converted the output frame size using Frame Controls, the Geometry parameters (see Lesson 8) can be set to 100 percent of the source. This process retains all of the image quality but realizes a benefit in efficiency because the time-consuming Frame Controls are encoded only once.

Think of job chaining as a form of assembly-line encoding that lets you control the stacking order of encoding tasks based on necessity or personal preference. For example, you may want to encode all frame rate conversions or reverse telecine transcodes before processing any frame size transformations. Using job chaining, you can parse and establish the task order by controlling the encoding within each of the steps. In essence, each job in the chain becomes a part of the larger job of outputting the final movie.

Using Batch Monitor

Batch Monitor is a separate application that you can open when Compressor submits a batch for encoding. It provides real-time feedback on the status of the currently encoding jobs and lists any jobs pending in the batch.

By default, Compressor does not automatically open Batch Monitor because the History window provides a basic view of the currently encoding batches and any batches that have been processed (see Lesson 1). Batch Monitor will open automatically if you choose Compressor > Preferences and select the "Auto launch Batch Monitor" checkbox.

When you first submit a job from the Batch window, a drop-down window opens to permit some last-minute adjustments before the job goes to processing.

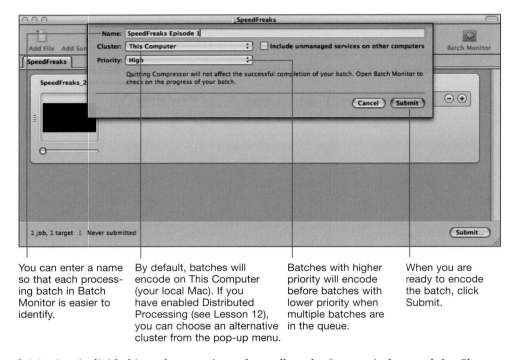

You can enter a name so that each processing batch in Batch Monitor is easier to identify.

By default, batches will encode on This Computer (your local Mac). If you have enabled Distributed Processing (see Lesson 12), you can choose an alternative cluster from the pop-up menu.

Batches with higher priority will encode before batches with lower priority when multiple batches are in the queue.

When you are ready to encode the batch, click Submit.

Batch Monitor is divided into three sections: the toolbar, the Status window, and the Cluster window. Each of these sections provides two functions: monitoring and management.

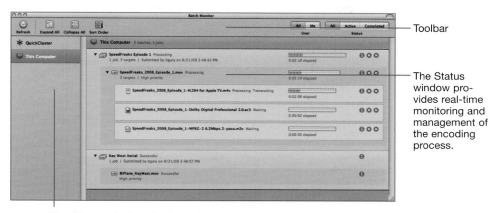

Toolbar

The Status window provides real-time monitoring and management of the encoding process.

The Cluster window displays all available clusters that you can monitor. Selecting a cluster in the list will display its batches in the Status window. This Computer is the default cluster that Batch Monitor oversees.

The toolbar controls how batches display in the Status window. You can modify which icons appear in the toolbar by choosing View > Customize Toolbar, or you can Control-click the toolbar and choose Customize Toolbar from the shortcut menu. From the drop-down window, drag desired items to the toolbar.

Click to manually refresh the Status window. By default, it will refresh automatically every five seconds.

Click to collapse all the batches in the Status window.

These buttons control which user's jobs are displayed in the Status window.

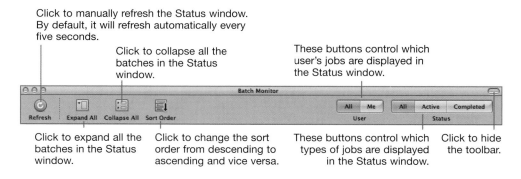

Click to expand all the batches in the Status window.

Click to change the sort order from descending to ascending and vice versa.

These buttons control which types of jobs are displayed in the Status window.

Click to hide the toolbar.

TIP ▶ To change the automatic refresh duration, choose Batch Monitor > Preferences and enter a new value in the "Update every" field.

In addition to displaying information on currently encoding batches and jobs, the Status window lets you manage the encoding process. The three buttons to the right of each batch and each job provide information as well as the ability to pause and cancel processes.

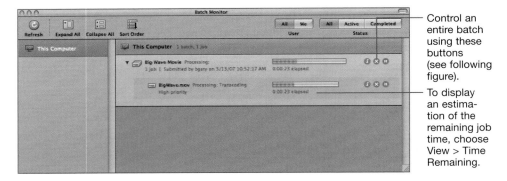

Control an entire batch using these buttons (see following figure).

To display an estimation of the remaining job time, choose View > Time Remaining.

Each individual job has its own set of buttons to control the encoding process.

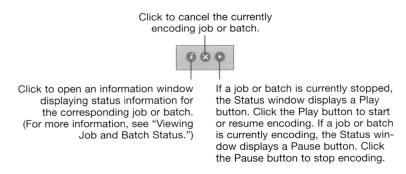

Click to cancel the currently encoding job or batch.

Click to open an information window displaying status information for the corresponding job or batch. (For more information, see "Viewing Job and Batch Status.")

If a job or batch is currently stopped, the Status window displays a Play button. Click the Play button to start or resume encoding. If a job or batch is currently encoding, the Status window displays a Pause button. Click the Pause button to stop encoding.

Some restrictions apply to starting and stopping encoding jobs and batches in the Batch Monitor. Some codecs, such as MPEG-2, allow you to pause and then resume processing from the point at which the encoding stopped. Other codecs, such as H.264, only let you stop processing and then force the encoder to restart the job from the beginning when encoding resumes.

If the job or batch you are attempting to stop will be affected by a total loss of currently encoded material, then after clicking the Pause button you will receive this alert from the Batch Monitor:

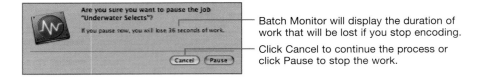

Batch Monitor will display the duration of work that will be lost if you stop encoding.

Click Cancel to continue the process or click Pause to stop the work.

Viewing Job and Batch Status

When you click the Information button, it opens an Information window for that job or batch.

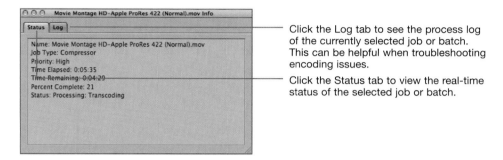

Click the Log tab to see the process log of the currently selected job or batch. This can be helpful when troubleshooting encoding issues.

Click the Status tab to view the real-time status of the selected job or batch.

To evaluate your understanding of the concepts covered in this lesson and to prepare for the Apple Pro Certification Exam, download the online quiz at www.peachpit.com/apts.compressor.

4

Core Concepts

- Choose encoding settings and create your own
- Choose and create destinations for encoded media
- Create Droplets to save time on repetitive tasks
- Work with Job Actions

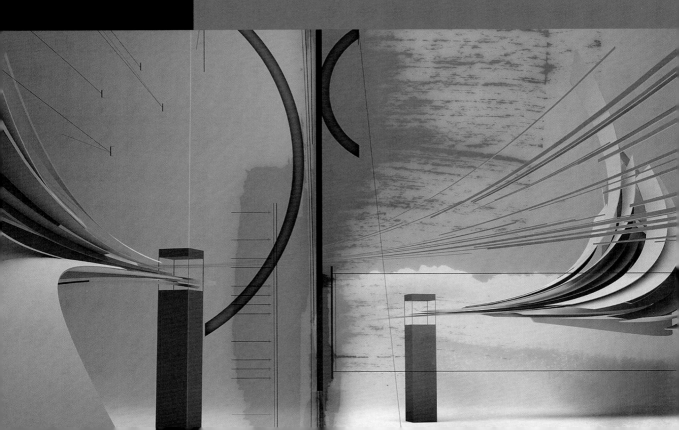

Working with Settings, Destinations, and Actions

The previous lesson discussed importing source media and managing the flow of jobs within the batches. This lesson will detail targets, which consist of settings and destinations, and it will also cover actions that Compressor can apply after processing completes.

Using Settings

Compressor installs with a series of predefined parameter files called settings that control the encoder and the output file destination. You can also create your own settings and destinations presets by modifying the Apple settings or by creating entirely new settings.

By default, the Settings window is a container for both the Settings and Destinations tabs. This default configuration keeps both of these preset groups in one convenient place.

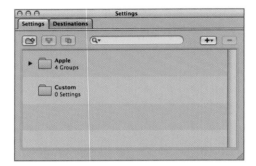

The title bar of the Settings window displays the currently active tab. In this example, the Settings tab is selected and therefore its name is displayed in the title bar.

Choosing Settings

Compressor encodes source media according to a collection of parameters and options known as a *setting*. Compressor installs a library of Apple settings for the most common digital media distribution platforms. These settings are divided into four groups: Apple Devices, DVD, Formats, and Other Workflows.

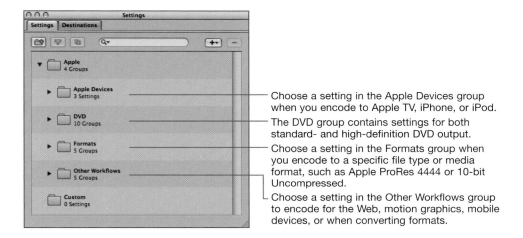

Choose a setting in the Apple Devices group when you encode to Apple TV, iPhone, or iPod.

The DVD group contains settings for both standard- and high-definition DVD output.

Choose a setting in the Formats group when you encode to a specific file type or media format, such as Apple ProRes 4444 or 10-bit Uncompressed.

Choose a setting in the Other Workflows group to encode for the Web, motion graphics, mobile devices, or when converting formats.

NOTE ► Some overlap does exist between groups. For example, Apple ProRes (HQ) can be found in both the Formats and Other Workflows groups.

Within each group, a hierarchy of folders is increasingly platform specific as you navigate through the path to an individual setting.

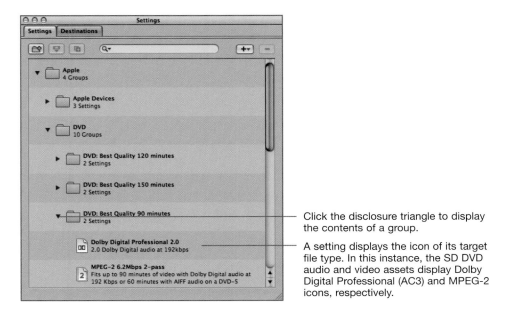

Click the disclosure triangle to display the contents of a group.

A setting displays the icon of its target file type. In this instance, the SD DVD audio and video assets display Dolby Digital Professional (AC3) and MPEG-2 icons, respectively.

Choosing Settings in the Inspector

Settings remain dormant until you either add them to a job in the Batch window—a target—or interact with them in the Inspector window (refer to Lesson 1 for information on the Inspector).

Select a setting or group from the list to open it in the Inspector window

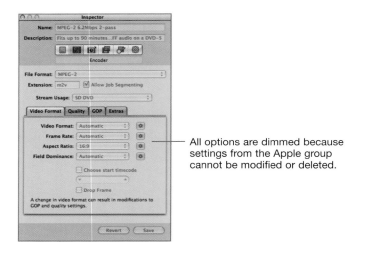

All options are dimmed because settings from the Apple group cannot be modified or deleted.

In this example, the summary tab of the Inspector window displays the information of the currently selected group.

The Encoder pane of the Inspector window displays the core parameters of each setting, and depending on the exact setting you select, the Encoder pane will display one of three templates:

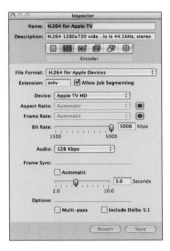

This display, with a combination of buttons, sliders, and pop-up menus, shows all available parameters within the same pane.

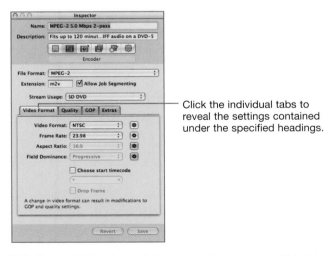

Click the individual tabs to reveal the settings contained under the specified headings.

This display divides the available parameters among multiple tabs.

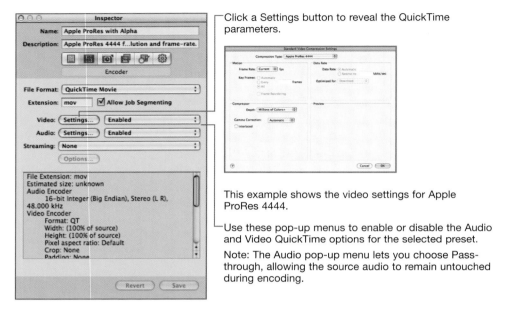

Click a Settings button to reveal the QuickTime parameters.

This example shows the video settings for Apple ProRes 4444.

Use these pop-up menus to enable or disable the Audio and Video QuickTime options for the selected preset.

Note: The Audio pop-up menu lets you choose Pass-through, allowing the source audio to remain untouched during encoding.

This display serves as a launching pad to the QuickTime interface windows that contain all the available settings.

Searching for Settings

The Apple settings in the Settings window have a logical organization by encoded file type or output media. For example, you'll obviously find settings for creating the requisite files for DVD authoring in the Apple > DVD group. However, some settings are buried a bit deeper in the folder structure. For example, to locate Apple ProRes 422 (Proxy) you'd navigate to Apple > Formats > QuickTime.

You don't have to know exactly where a setting is located or its exact name to find it. The Settings window has a dynamic search field that lets you enter words and phrases to narrow down the list of settings.

For example, typing *Apple ProRes* in the field returns the following list:

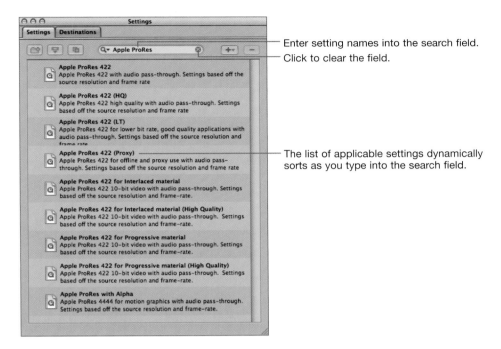

Enter setting names into the search field.

Click to clear the field.

The list of applicable settings dynamically sorts as you type into the search field.

Compressor searches both the names and the descriptions of settings when performing searches. For example, typing *dvcam* returns these results:

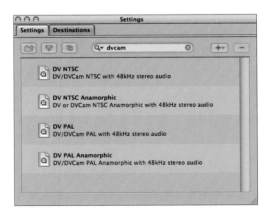

TIP ▶ If you don't know the file type or setting you're looking for, but you know the type of media you ultimately want to produce, try using the batch template workflow described in Lesson 2.

Applying Settings to Jobs

When settings are applied to jobs in the Batch window, they create targets that comprise a setting, a destination, and an output filename. Jobs in the Batch window can have a single target or multiple targets applied to them.

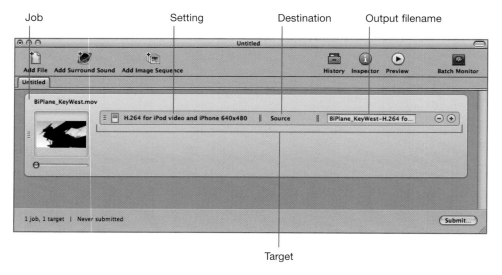

In the Batch windows, you can apply settings to jobs using one of the following three methods:

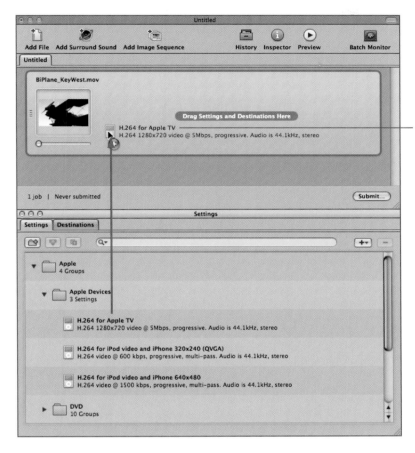

The simplest way to apply a setting to a job in the Batch window is to drag the desired setting or setting group from the Settings window onto a job.

When you add a setting group (folder), all of the settings in the group are applied as targets.

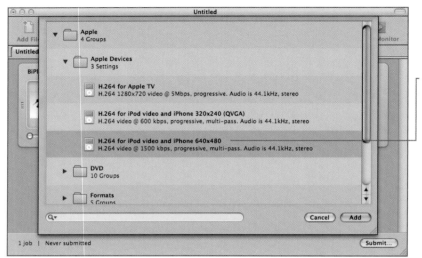

Select a job in the Batch window and choose Target > New Target With Setting. In this drop-down window, navigate to the desired setting, choose it, and click Add.

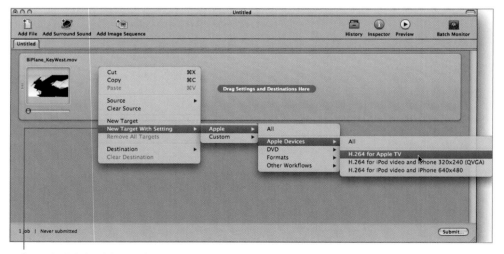

Control-click (or right-click) a job in the Batch window and choose New Target With Setting from the shortcut menu. Navigate through the submenus and choose the desired setting.

TIP Choosing All in any of the submenus will apply all of the settings contained within that group.

Modifying the Apple Settings

The most convenient way to create a custom setting is to duplicate an Apple setting and then save the modifications as a unique preset.

If, for example, your movie is intended to become bonus material on an SD DVD, you could duplicate an Apple SD DVD setting, which will create an MPEG-2 setting in the Custom folder with the suffix "Copy" appended. Then you can adjust that setting as needed and save it.

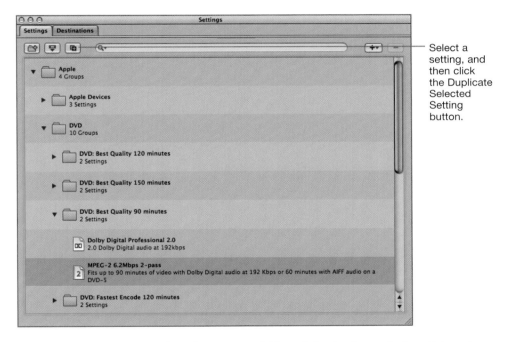

Select a setting, and then click the Duplicate Selected Setting button.

A new custom setting is created in the Custom folder of the Settings window. Select the new custom setting to load it into the Inspector.

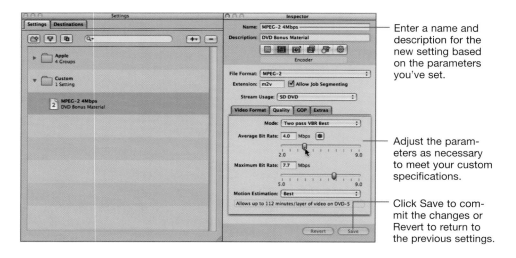

Enter a name and description for the new setting based on the parameters you've set.

Adjust the parameters as necessary to meet your custom specifications.

Click Save to commit the changes or Revert to return to the previous settings.

NOTE ▶ The Apple settings cannot be modified or deleted.

Saving Temporary Modifications to Settings

In addition to duplicating a setting in the Settings window, you can apply a setting to a job, modify the target, and then save those modifications as a new custom setting.

Selecting the target opens it in the Inspector window

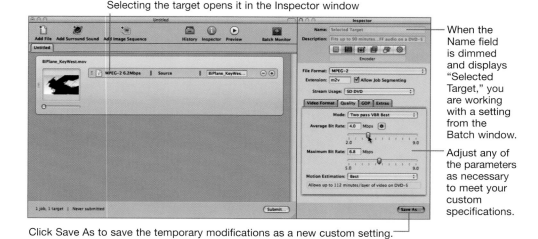

When the Name field is dimmed and displays "Selected Target," you are working with a setting from the Batch window.

Adjust any of the parameters as necessary to meet your custom specifications.

Click Save As to save the temporary modifications as a new custom setting.

NOTE ► When you add a setting to a job in the Batch window and create a target, Compressor uses a copy of the setting, not the setting itself. Therefore, any changes you make to settings applied to jobs in the Batch window will not alter the original settings in the Settings window.

If you make any modifications that would work well for future encoding sessions, be sure to save them because after a batch is submitted for encoding, the setting reverts to its original parameters in the Settings window and any modifications are discarded.

TIP ► In the event that you forgot to save a modified target, you can reload the batch from the History window (see Lesson 1) into the Batch window and save the customized target.

In addition to displaying in the Settings window, custom settings will appear in the Custom folder of the target drop-down window, and in the Batch window in the New Target With Setting submenu of the shortcut menu.

NOTE ► The target from which the new custom setting was derived can be further modified without changing the settings of the new custom preset because they are all separate files.

Creating Custom Presets

Creating custom settings presets requires just a few additional steps and a little planning.

First, decide what type of encoding process the preset should address. Compressor offers the following options for custom settings:

Export Option	Primary Use
AIFF	Uncompressed PCM audio for DVD or audio CD
DV Stream	Encoding for use in iMovie
Dolby Digital Professional	Compressed audio for DVDs. Compressor can produce both 2.0- and 5.1-format files.

Export Option	Primary Use
H.264 for Apple Devices	High-quality video for iPods, iPhones, and Apple TV
H.264 for DVD Studio Pro	High-definition video assets for high-definition disc delivery
H.264 for Blu-ray	High-definition video elementary stream for Blu-ray Disc authoring
Image Sequence	Creates a sequence of still images from the source media; used primarily for CGI work
MP3	Compressed audio for Internet delivery and podcasting
MPEG-1	Lower-quality/lower-bandwidth codec often used for VCD and cross-platform web delivery
MPEG-2	Standard video encoder for SD DVD and HD discs
MPEG-4	Produces high-quality web media at relatively fast encoding times; requires QuickTime 6 or later for playback (Mac or PC)
QuickTime Export Components	Suitable for cell-phone (3G) delivery or any third-party plug-in that is Compressor compatible
QuickTime Movie	Creates QuickTime container files with any of the available audio or video codecs

You create custom settings directly in the Settings window.

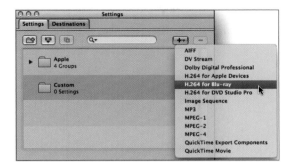

Click the "Create a new setting" button and choose an export option based on the previous table.

Custom settings appear in the Custom folder.

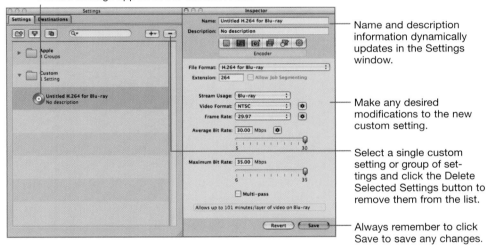

Name and description information dynamically updates in the Settings window.

Make any desired modifications to the new custom setting.

Select a single custom setting or group of settings and click the Delete Selected Settings button to remove them from the list.

Always remember to click Save to save any changes.

NOTE ▸ Unlike Apple settings, custom settings are fully editable in the Inspector window. Select any setting in the Custom folder, make the desired changes in the Inspector, and then click Save.

Organizing Custom Settings

Custom settings can be organized into specialized folders and applied to a job as a group, just like Apple settings.

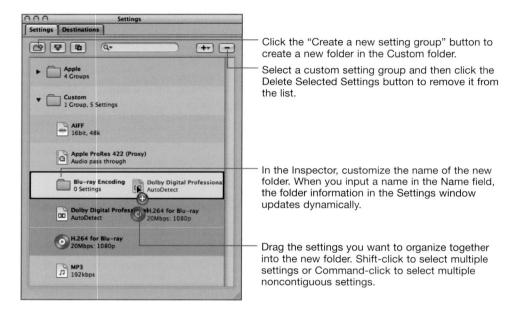

Click the "Create a new setting group" button to create a new folder in the Custom folder.

Select a custom setting group and then click the Delete Selected Settings button to remove it from the list.

In the Inspector, customize the name of the new folder. When you input a name in the Name field, the folder information in the Settings window updates dynamically.

Drag the settings you want to organize together into the new folder. Shift-click to select multiple settings or Command-click to select multiple noncontiguous settings.

TIP You can also delete custom settings or groups of settings by selecting them in the Settings window and pressing the Delete key.

The settings you've organized together can all be applied to a job by dragging the group folder from the Settings window onto the job in the Batch window.

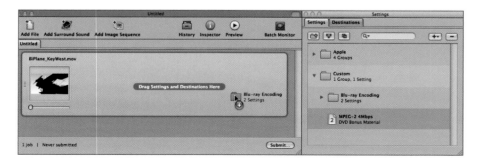

NOTE ► Custom settings and groups are also available in the drop-down window after choosing Target > New Target With Setting, and in the shortcut menu in the Batch window.

Using Automatic Settings

Some settings have automatic aspects to their encoder parameters. For example, you can allow Compressor to define a series of settings in the encoder pane of MPEG-2 presets based on its analysis of the source media.

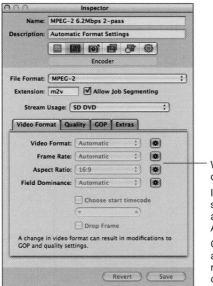

When you engage automatic options, Compressor dims the corresponding menus.

In this example, based on its analysis of the source media, Compressor will automatically assign the values for Video Format, Frame Rate, Aspect Ratio, and Field Dominance.

Clicking the button turns the automatic option on and off. When an automatic option is off, the corresponding menu will activate and you may then choose a custom setting from the available options.

TIP ► It's good practice to open source media in the Inspector window (see Lesson 1) to ensure that Compressor has analyzed the clip properly. If Compressor's analysis is incorrect or the source media contains nonstandard metadata, turn off the automatic options and manually enter the values for any applied targets.

Auto Detect Settings

You can drop a QuickTime movie onto the Custom folder of the Settings window and Compressor will define a brand new custom setting based on the metadata it finds in the encoded file.

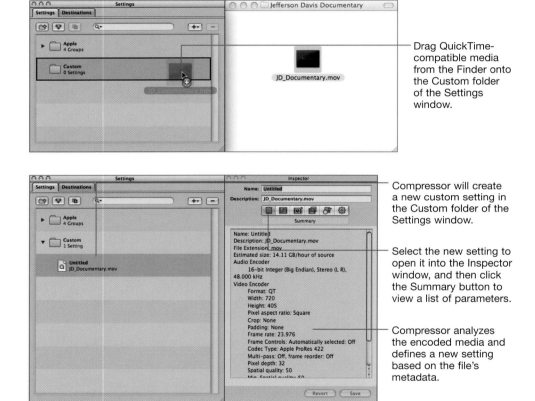

Drag QuickTime-compatible media from the Finder onto the Custom folder of the Settings window.

Compressor will create a new custom setting in the Custom folder of the Settings window.

Select the new setting to open it into the Inspector window, and then click the Summary button to view a list of parameters.

Compressor analyzes the encoded media and defines a new setting based on the file's metadata.

Use the Auto Detect Settings feature as a starting point for creating your own custom settings; but be aware that the results—especially for media not encoded by Compressor—may vary or not produce a viable preset for subsequent encoding.

TIP ▶ If you've previously encoded media with Compressor using a temporary modification of a target, but failed to save those changes as a new custom setting, you can use the Auto Detect Settings feature on the output media and create a new setting based on the encoded file.

Using Destinations

Destinations are a second, very important part of a target because they tell Compressor where to output the encoded media.

Source (the same folder where the input media originated) is the default destination that Compressor automatically applies to new targets.

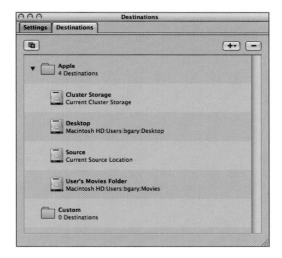

Compressor installs with four destination presets.

NOTE ▶ The root of the startup disk is the Source destination for targets applied to jobs with Final Cut Pro sequences as the source media.

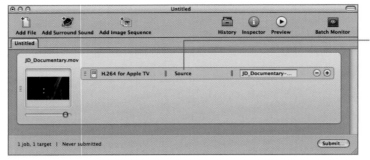

The middle entry of the target displays the destination. In this example, the output file will be saved to the same folder as the source media.

Note: You can change the default destination by changing the Default Destination setting in Compressor's preferences.

Modifying a Target's Destination

Compressor offers three ways to change a target's output location from the default destination:

Control-click the target and choose Destination from the shortcut menu. Then, choose a location from the submenu.

Choose Other to display the Open drop-down window in which you can navigate to a temporary destination for this target.

You can also modify the destination by selecting a target, choosing Target > Destination, and then selecting the output location from the options in the list. Choose Other to define a custom destination for the selected target.

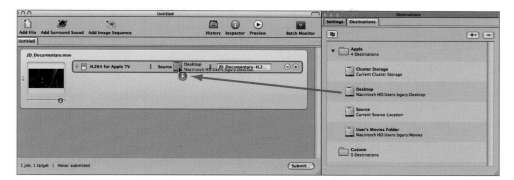

Drag a destination from the Settings window directly onto a target.

With the target selected, choose Target > Destination and choose a location from the submenu.

Creating Custom Destinations

You can create permanent custom destinations in the Destinations tab of the Settings window by modifying existing destinations or creating new destinations based on a local or remote output location. Local destinations are storage devices connected to your computer, whereas remote locations are devices that you connect to via a network (file server) or the Internet (such as an FTP site or MobileMe account).

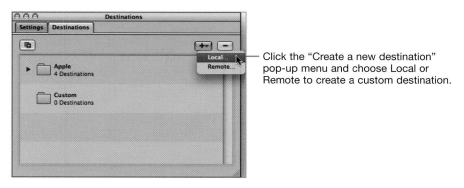

Click the "Create a new destination" pop-up menu and choose Local or Remote to create a custom destination.

As with settings, custom destinations that you create will appear in the Custom folder. You can apply custom destinations to jobs just as you apply Apple destinations.

Choosing Local Destinations

When you choose Local, an Open drop-down window appears in which you can choose the output location on a drive or device directly connected to your computer. Navigate to the desired location and click Open.

The new custom destination will appear in the Custom folder. In the Inspector window, name the destination and modify its properties.

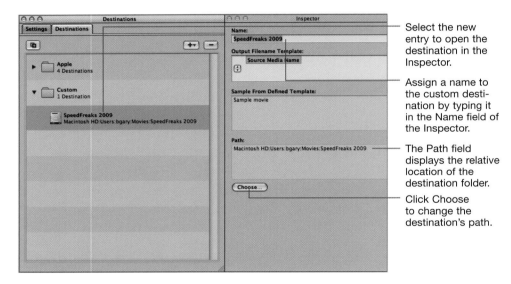

Select the new entry to open the destination in the Inspector.

Assign a name to the custom destination by typing it in the Name field of the Inspector.

The Path field displays the relative location of the destination folder.

Click Choose to change the destination's path.

You can use the Output Filename Template field and pop-up menu to modify which suffixes Compressor appends to the output filename. The default export option only uses the source media's name and the target file extension. For example, if your source media is a DV NTSC clip with a filename of My Movie.mov, and you apply an Apple TV target, the output filename would be My Movie.m4v.

You may find that placing more information in the filename is useful when outputting to custom destinations. For example, you can append the current date to the filename to aid the organization of multiple encoding jobs.

TIP ▸ When creating files for use in DVD Studio Pro, avoid using any identifier other than the source media name. DVD Studio Pro will combine similarly named audio and video elementary streams as a single unit inside the application. For example, the files MyAwesomeMovie.m2v and MyAwesomeMovie.ac3 would be paired by DVD Studio Pro even though they were separate assets. Creating a custom destination just for this purpose is a handy, timesaving trick because it avoids manually assigning paired assets during authoring.

Choosing Remote Destinations

When you choose Remote, a drop-down window appears in which you can input all of your server connection information.

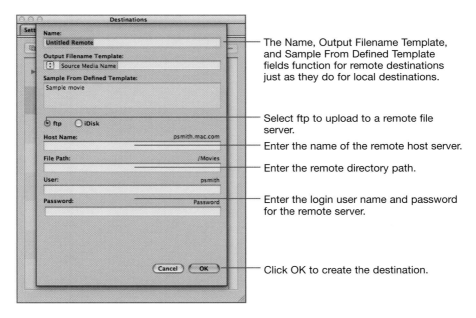

The Name, Output Filename Template, and Sample From Defined Template fields function for remote destinations just as they do for local destinations.

Select ftp to upload to a remote file server.

Enter the name of the remote host server.

Enter the remote directory path.

Enter the login user name and password for the remote server.

Click OK to create the destination.

Consult your network or site administrator for login information.

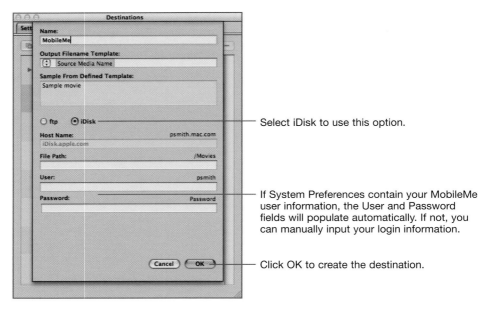

Select iDisk to use this option.

If System Preferences contain your MobileMe user information, the User and Password fields will populate automatically. If not, you can manually input your login information.

Click OK to create the destination.

If you have a MobileMe account, you can create a destination that will upload directly to your online storage.

Working with Droplets

When settings grow up and graduate, they become Droplets. Compressor uses Droplets to pack settings into an application suitcase so they can stand alone in the Finder and run entirely outside Compressor.

You can create Droplets from any Apple or custom setting in the Settings window and then drag QuickTime-compatible media onto them to start encoding. Droplets can be quite handy, especially for repetitive encoding tasks in which settings do not change from job to job.

> **NOTE** ▶ Compressor and Qmaster must be installed on any system to which you intend to use Droplets. It's also good practice to verify that the same version of Compressor is installed on each computer you intend to run the Droplets to ensure compatibility.

Creating Droplets

You can create Droplets in Compressor in one of two ways. The method you choose mainly depends on where you're working and what you're currently doing.

If you're currently working with a setting in the Settings window that would make a good Droplet, select it and then click the "Save Selection as Droplet" button.

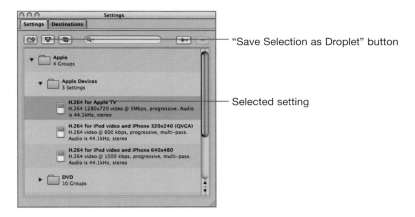

The settings in the Apple Devices group are good candidates for promotion to Droplets because in most cases they're applied to jobs with no customization; that is, the parameters are already tuned for Apple devices, and the automatic options allow for variances from source to source.

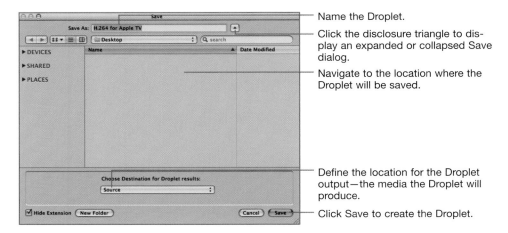

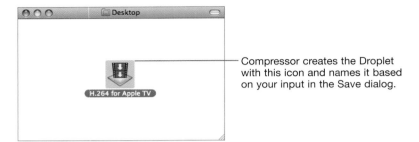

Compressor creates the Droplet with this icon and names it based on your input in the Save dialog.

Compressor saves the setting to the directed location as a stand-alone application.

Drag QuickTime-compatible media onto the Droplet to begin the encoding process; you can drop a single file or multiple files concurrently.

> **NOTE ▸** When dropping several hundred files (or a few very large files) onto a Droplet at once, you may experience a long delay before the application opens. To avoid this delay, parse your source media into smaller groups and drag them onto the Droplet separately.

The Droplet connects to the Compressor transcoder (background service) and opens the Droplet window, which displays all the options and parameters.

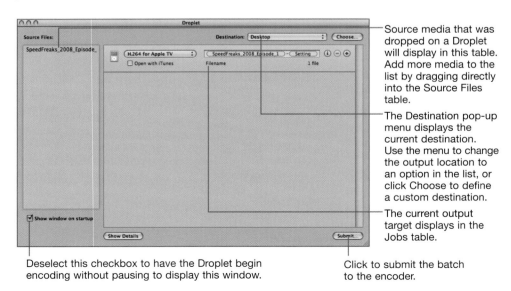

Source media that was dropped on a Droplet will display in this table. Add more media to the list by dragging directly into the Source Files table.

The Destination pop-up menu displays the current destination. Use the menu to change the output location to an option in the list, or click Choose to define a custom destination.

The current output target displays in the Jobs table.

Deselect this checkbox to have the Droplet begin encoding without pausing to display this window.

Click to submit the batch to the encoder.

The Job Type pop-up menu displays the active target.

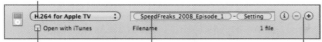

Certain targets may have available actions that can be engaged by selecting this checkbox.

Output filename template; manually edit any section of name by double-clicking it.

These buttons add and delete jobs to the Droplet.

Note: Droplets must contain at least one job. The Minus (-) button will be dimmed if only one job remains.

Click the Information button to display a pop-up window with details about the current job.

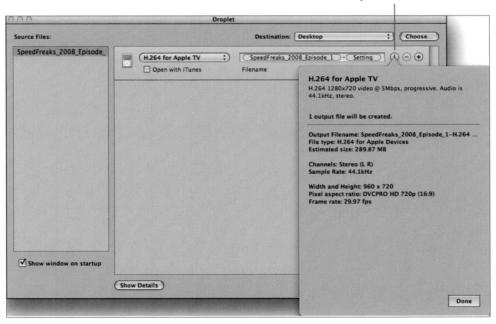

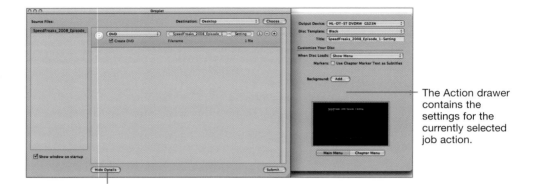

The Action drawer contains the settings for the currently selected job action.

Click the Show Details button to display the Action drawer.
Click Hide Details to close the drawer.

An alternative way to produce a Droplet is to choose File > Create Droplet and define the application parameters in the Save dialog that opens.

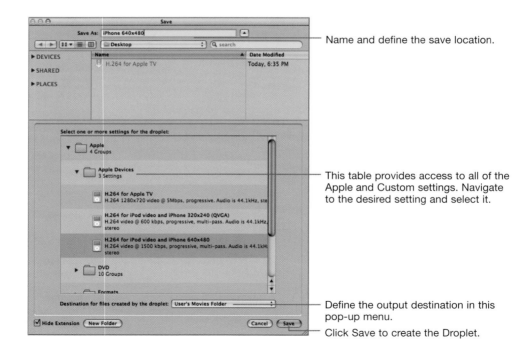

Name and define the save location.

This table provides access to all of the Apple and Custom settings. Navigate to the desired setting and select it.

Define the output destination in this pop-up menu.

Click Save to create the Droplet.

Managing Multiple Settings in Droplets

When creating a Droplet, you can include single or multiple settings. Alternatively, you can add settings and templates to a completed Droplet in its main window.

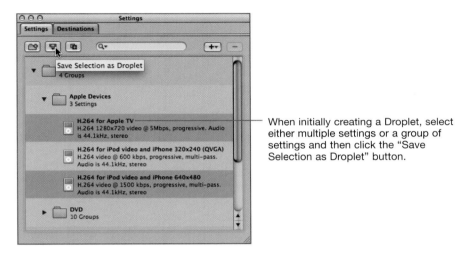

When initially creating a Droplet, select either multiple settings or a group of settings and then click the "Save Selection as Droplet" button.

In the Save dialog that opens, define the Name, Save Location, and Output Media Destination and then click Save to create the Droplet.

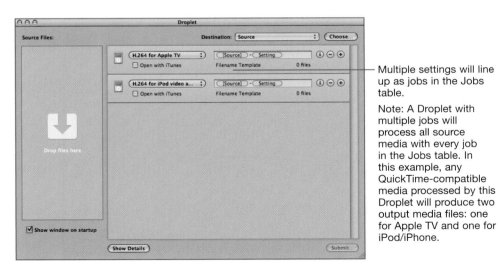

Multiple settings will line up as jobs in the Jobs table.

Note: A Droplet with multiple jobs will process all source media with every job in the Jobs table. In this example, any QuickTime-compatible media processed by this Droplet will produce two output media files: one for Apple TV and one for iPod/iPhone.

You can also add jobs directly to an open Droplet by clicking an existing job's Plus (+) button in the Jobs table.

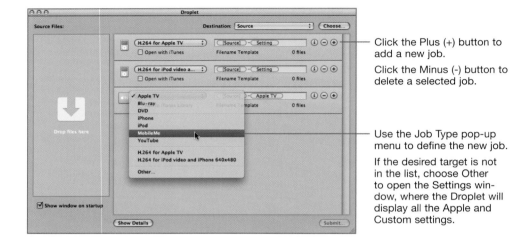

Click the Plus (+) button to add a new job.

Click the Minus (-) button to delete a selected job.

Use the Job Type pop-up menu to define the new job.

If the desired target is not in the list, choose Other to open the Settings window, where the Droplet will display all the Apple and Custom settings.

Modifying Droplets

Droplets dynamically save any modifications you make to them while their windows are open. The Undo and Redo commands in the Edit menu are not available when working with Droplets, so be cautious when changing the Jobs table or the Destination settings. You can duplicate a Droplet at the Finder level and make any changes to the copy to ensure that the original version remains unchanged.

To close an open Droplet, choose Droplet > Quit Droplet.

> **NOTE ▶** Only one Droplet may be open at a time. To make changes to another Droplet, first quit the currently open Droplet, and from the Finder, double-click another Droplet to interact with its window.

Working with Actions

Actions occur after Compressor processes the media. They perform tasks such as burning DVDs and Blu-ray Discs, uploading movies to MobileMe and YouTube, and running AppleScripts or Automator actions. Compressor contains two types of actions: *job* and *setting*.

Using Job Actions

Lesson 2 covers job actions and batch templates in detail, but here are some general considerations when working with these types of post-transcoding tasks.

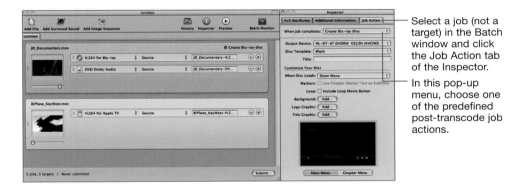

Select a job (not a target) in the Batch window and click the Job Action tab of the Inspector.

In this pop-up menu, choose one of the predefined post-transcode job actions.

> **TIP** ▶ Compressor Help defines each of the job actions in detail.

The Run Automator Workflow job action, though seemingly simple, is quite powerful.

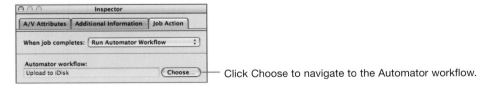

Click Choose to navigate to the Automator workflow.

Automator-created scripts can significantly increase your productivity and efficiency in a wide variety of tasks and functions. For more information on Automator and scripting applications and Mac OS X, go to www.macosxautomation.com/automator/.

Resolving Conflicts with Job Actions

Compressor will display alerts and warnings if you attempt to configure a specific job action with incompatible targets.

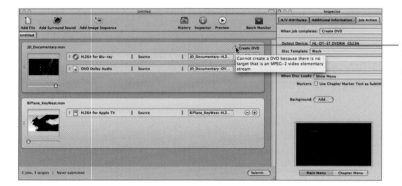

Hover the mouse over the alert triangle to display the message.

In this example, the job action is set to DVD, but the targets are set to create incompatible Blu-ray Disc media. To fix this situation, you would either change the job action to burn a Blu-ray Disc or apply the correct DVD targets.

Using Settings Actions

Settings actions let you send a post-transcode email to a single recipient or to run a single AppleScript after encoding is completed. Both actions are linked directly to a specific setting, and you control these tasks in the Actions pane of the Inspector.

Before enabling email notification, you must configure Compressor's preferences by choosing Compressor > Preferences.

> **TIP** You can set email notification or script execution for each job in a batch by configuring the Actions pane for each individual setting. As Compressor completes each job in the list, it will send an email or run a script.

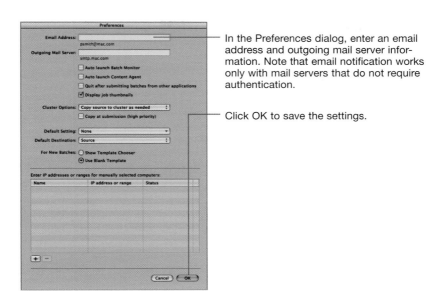

In the Preferences dialog, enter an email address and outgoing mail server information. Note that email notification works only with mail servers that do not require authentication.

Click OK to save the settings.

NOTE ▶ You may need to restart Compressor for the new preferences to take effect.

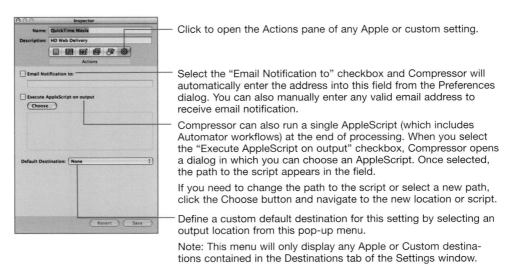

Click to open the Actions pane of any Apple or custom setting.

Select the "Email Notification to" checkbox and Compressor will automatically enter the address into this field from the Preferences dialog. You can also manually enter any valid email address to receive email notification.

Compressor can also run a single AppleScript (which includes Automator workflows) at the end of processing. When you select the "Execute AppleScript on output" checkbox, Compressor opens a dialog in which you can choose an AppleScript. Once selected, the path to the script appears in the field.

If you need to change the path to the script or select a new path, click the Choose button and navigate to the new location or script.

Define a custom default destination for this setting by selecting an output location from this pop-up menu.

Note: This menu will only display any Apple or Custom destinations contained in the Destinations tab of the Settings window.

To evaluate your understanding of the concepts covered in this lesson and to prepare for the Apple Pro Certification Exam, download the online quiz at www.peachpit.com/apts.compressor.

5

Core Concepts

Use the Preview window to audition input and output media

Use real-time previews to audition Filter and Geometry settings

Output test clips to preview Encoder and Frame Control settings

Lesson 5
Test Clip Workflows

Compressor allows you to create and efficiently organize a series of encoding jobs and then process them unattended. This works especially well if you are comfortable with your encoder settings and have confidence in the output file quality.

But what do you do when you are not sure of the final quality or you want to experiment with different targets to find the perfect match for your source media? Encoding multiple test compressions of a two-hour movie is not an efficient use of your time. Fortunately, Compressor supports real-time previews and test-render workflows that accurately represent the final output quality without requiring you to encode the entire source media.

Viewing Real-Time Previews

The Preview window displays real-time playback of source media originating from QuickTime files, Motion projects, or Final Cut Pro sequences. Additionally, target settings applied to source media will play back in real time with some limitations. Selecting source media or targets in the Batch window automatically loads the content into an active Preview window. If the Preview window is currently closed, choose Window > Preview or click the Preview button on the Batch window toolbar.

Jump the playhead to a specific timecode by entering it into the timecode field. The up- and down-pointing triangles move the playhead forward and backward one frame at a time. See below for more details.

Click the Preview Scale pop-up menu to set the relative window size based on the pixel dimensions of the source media. Note that this setting has no effect on output file dimensions.

Compressor displays the frame size and rate of the source media here.

Use the transport controls to preview the media. In addition to using the transport controls, you can press the Left or Right Arrow keys to move the playhead forward or backward one frame at a time.

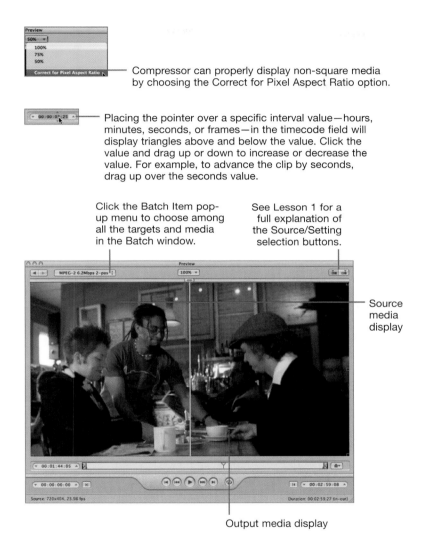

Compressor can properly display non-square media by choosing the Correct for Pixel Aspect Ratio option.

Placing the pointer over a specific interval value—hours, minutes, seconds, or frames—in the timecode field will display triangles above and below the value. Click the value and drag up or down to increase or decrease the value. For example, to advance the clip by seconds, drag up over the seconds value.

Click the Batch Item pop-up menu to choose among all the targets and media in the Batch window.

See Lesson 1 for a full explanation of the Source/Setting selection buttons.

Source media display

Output media display

NOTE ▶ The Preview window will display only Filters and Geometry settings during realtime playback. To see Encoder or Frame Controls settings use the Test Clip workflow described in the following section.

Drag the slider to the left or right to preview different
sections of the media with the applied target. Move
the slider during pause or playback. Compressor will
dynamically adjust the real-time preview.

The presence of the Split Screen slider indicates that a target is
loaded into the Preview window.

Compressor can work with Final Cut Pro to encode sequences in the background, but
only one at a time. This dialog will appear if you attempt to access a Final Cut Pro batch
in the Preview window, while another sequence is processing:

Encoding Test Clips

Viewing real-time previews on your computer screen is especially useful for testing settings destined for formats that use the RGB color space, such as movies for the web or
Apple devices. Non-RGB formats such as Blu-ray Disc or DVD, however, are often best
tested in their native environments to verify output quality. During the encoding process,

you can significantly improve your efficiency, as well as your quality control, by applying targets to small sections of the source media, encoding the batch, and then burning the results to optical media for playback. Test encoding 30 to 60 seconds of the source is often more than enough material to evaluate settings that, once approved, can then be applied to the entire source media—and it is much faster than processing a full 30- to 60-minute movie.

Testing a Single Section

The first step when creating test clips is to define the section of the imported source media that you want to encode with single or multiple target settings.

Import source media and apply as many targets as you would like to test. In this example, three different web delivery targets are applied.

Next, select the job—not any of the targets—to load it into the Preview window. Use the Preview window to set In and Out points that limit the duration of the test range; by default, all clips have their In and Out points set at the beginning and the end of the media.

> **TIP** The fastest way to set In and Out points is to scrub the playhead to your desired In point location and press I on the keyboard to set the In point. Set the Out point by scrubbing the playhead and pressing O at the desired end frame.

The absence of the Split Screen slider indicates that source media is loaded into the Preview window.

Once you have applied targets to test in the Batch window and have defined the output clip's duration in the Preview window, you can submit the entire batch for encoding.

Use the Timecode field to find the exact frames for the In and Out points, either by manually entering the timecode or by clicking the triangles at each end of the field to move the playhead forward or backward one frame at at time.

In and Out range defines which section of the media will be sent to the encoder.

The Duration readout displays the current length of the media between the In and Out points.

When the playhead is parked on the desired start location, click this button to set an In point. The timecode field to the left will display the In point timecode.

When the playhead is parked on the desired end location, click this button to set an Out point. The timecode field to the right will display the Out point timecode.

NOTE ► Finding the best settings for the output media may require creating several test clips.

When you have determined the final settings, re-import the job from the History window (for more information, see "Using the History Window" in this lesson). Use the target that produced the best output, and make sure that the In and Out points in the Preview window are placed at the beginning and end of the source media, otherwise you will encode only the test section of the source media. Choose an output destination, make any desired adjustments to the filename, and submit the batch for encoding.

NOTE ► When you re-import a batch from the History window, all of its jobs and associated targets are also imported. You may need to remove any unwanted targets from the final batch before submitting it to the encoder.

Testing Multiple Sections

You may have source media that changes significantly throughout the program, so test-ing just one section may not provide a broad enough sample for you to make an accurate determination of a specific target's performance quality.

The trick is to apply the same target to different sections of the source media and then encode the different samples as one batch.

First, import source media.

Select and copy the job.

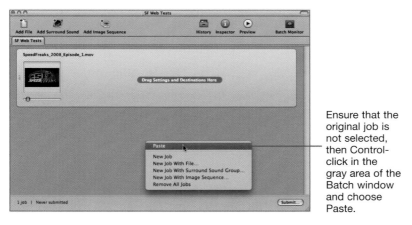

Ensure that the original job is not selected, then Control-click in the gray area of the Batch window and choose Paste.

If you have more than two sections to test, continue pasting the source media into the active Batch tab until you've created enough jobs to satisfy all the sections.

Select the first job to open it in the Preview window and then set In and Out points for the first section you want to test. Repeat this process for as many jobs as you want to test, each time defining a different section of the source media.

In this example, a high action shot and a static standup were defined as the test samples.

You can quickly apply the same target to several jobs in the batch by Command-clicking each job and then choosing Target > New Target With Setting. From the drop-down window, select the target and choose Add. When the batch is ready to encode, click Submit.

Managing Test Clips

Compressor also lets you independently apply multiple targets to each of the test jobs. You could even apply multiple targets to one job and a single target to all the others. The options are many and varied.

Because only 30- to 60-second sections are sent to the encoder, even complex batches compress quickly.

After you find the best target for your delivery requirements, the challenge is managing all the test clips so that you can easily return to Compressor and apply that test clip's target to the entire movie.

You can easily accomplish this by creating custom destinations (see Lesson 4) and custom presets (see Lesson 3) and modifying the output filenames so that each test is uniquely identified.

Using the History Window

The History window provides convenient access to previously encoded jobs and is particularly handy when encoding multiple test clips because you can drag the job that rendered the most successful output back into the Batch window for resubmission. You can also click the Magnifying Glass icon next to a particular job to view the output media in the Finder.

Drag batches directly from the History window into the Batch window.

When the batch is re-imported, delete the targets that did not meet your requirements. When you're ready to export the full source media, make sure to select the job—not one of the targets—and reset the In and Out points of the source media to the beginning and end of the entire clip.

> **TIP** ▶ You can expand or collapse batches in the History window by clicking the disclosure triangles or double-clicking the entries in the list.

To evaluate your understanding of the concepts covered in this lesson and to prepare for the Apple Pro Certification Exam, download the online quiz at www.peachpit.com/apts.compressor.

6

Core Concepts

Transcode video formats

Resize and retime video from one format to another

Converting with Frame Controls

Frame Controls let you augment the encoding process by implementing more advanced technology when converting from one video format to another. Frame Controls function as separate tasks during encoding, apart from the target's codec. You can control this added layer of processing by implementing the job chaining tactics discussed in Lesson 3.

Using Frame Controls

Frame Controls employ optical flow technology (also used in Apple's Shake, Motion, and Final Cut Pro), which calculates motion tracking for every pixel vector as it goes from one movie frame to the next. When that calculation is completed for a given frame rate and frame size, Compressor can intelligently place those pixels in different frame rates and sizes during a conversion. Compared to inferior conversion techniques like blending and scaling, optical flow produces amazing results, but the massive increases in quality come at the expense of longer encoding times.

Frame controls are most useful when you are converting from one video format (standard) to another and requires a change in frame size and/or rate, such as converting NTSC footage (720 x 480 at 25 fps) to PAL (720 x 546 at 29.97 fps) or downconverting high definition video to standard definition. Additionally, Frame Controls can greatly improve conversions between interlaced and progressive video along with removing film to video pulldown, also known as *reverse telecine*. You can achieve broadcast-level transcoding in Compressor, but as a general rule, when working with Frame Controls, you have to choose between higher quality and faster encoding.

> **TIP** ▶ Frame Controls *cannot* be viewed in the Preview window. Use the Test Clip workflows (described in Lesson 6) to see the output of Frame Controls.

You access Frame Controls in the Inspector window by selecting a custom setting from the Settings window or a target from the Batch window.

Click the Frame Controls button to display the settings.

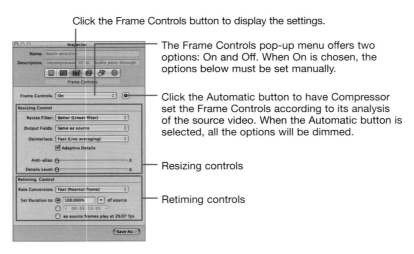

The Frame Controls pop-up menu offers two options: On and Off. When On is chosen, the options below must be set manually.

Click the Automatic button to have Compressor set the Frame Controls according to its analysis of the source video. When the Automatic button is selected, all the options will be dimmed.

Resizing controls

Retiming controls

NOTE ▶ The automatic option works in only two instances: when downconverting HD content to SD MPEG-2, and when encoding in H.264 for Apple devices. For all other instances you will need to create custom settings. Deselect the Automatic button, and from the Frame Controls pop-up menu, choose On.

Resizing Controls

When source media is transformed from one frame size to another—in converting HD footage to SD, for example—the resizing controls can significantly increase the conversion quality.

The Output Fields and Deinterlace pop-up menus work together to control conversions between interlaced and progressive footage. If you choose "Same as source" in the Output Fields pop-up menu, no conversion will occur, and Compressor will ignore the Deinterlace option.

If you choose Progressive in the Output Fields pop-up menu and the source media is interlaced, the selection in the Deinterlace pop-up menu is applied. When converting progressive sources to interlaced formats, make sure to choose the correct field dominance (Top or Bottom) for the output format. Generally, the best choice in the Deinterlace pop-up menu is Better (Motion adaptive).

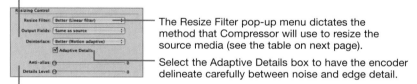

The Resize Filter pop-up menu dictates the method that Compressor will use to resize the source media (see the table on next page).

Select the Adaptive Details box to have the encoder delineate carefully between noise and edge detail.

The Anti-alias and Details Level sliders increase smoothness and sharpness within the frame size conversion. When source media is scaled up or down, jagged artifacting or detail blurring can occur in the transcoded media. Use the Anti-alias slider to smooth jagged edges, and use the Details Level slider to adjust image sharpness. Use the sliders independently or in tandem to achieve the desired results.

TIP ▶ Deselect the Adaptive Details box when encoding video for iPods, iPhones, computer monitors, or any other devices with progressive scan displays. Deselecting this box allows Compressor to utilize the same deinterlacing algorithms used by Apple's DVD Player. The resulting encoding times will be significantly shorter with the box deselected.

Quality vs. Encoding Time	Resize Filter Choice
Fastest encoding	Fast (Nearest pixel). Encoding calculations are based on a blending of relative pixel positions from frame to frame.
Balance between	Better (Linear filter). This option adds a weighted-speed and quality average calculation to the Fast method that produces much smoother results at the cost of increased encoding time. Use this option if motion artifacting is present when Fast is used.
Best quality	Best (Statistical Prediction). This option kicks optical flow into high gear, as it analyzes each frame pixel by pixel and reconstitutes frames mathematically by repositioning each pixel relative to the new frame size.

Reverse Telecine

When 24 fps film is transferred to video, it undergoes a process called telecine. During that process, extra frames are added to conform the 24 fps progressive footage into 29.97 fps interlaced video for playback in the NTSC format. This process is commonly referred to as a 3:2 pulldown. Compressor automatically detects the pulldown pattern of sources that have either constant or broken cadences and adjusts the processing as necessary. You can use Frame Controls to reverse that process (reverse telecine) and output 23.97-frame media from NTSC sources for editing in Final Cut Pro.

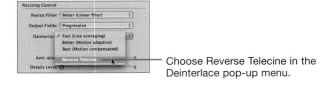

Choose Reverse Telecine in the Deinterlace pop-up menu.

NOTE ► When Reverse Telecine is selected, the other frame controls options are disabled.

TIP ► Do not segment Reverse Telecine jobs because the cadence detection may not be processed accurately.

Adding Pulldown

Compressor can also add a 3:2 pulldown to progressive sources, thereby creating 29.97 interlaced media.

To add the proper cadence you must define three settings:

Set the Frame Rate in the Encoder settings to an interlaced output: 29.97 or 59.94.

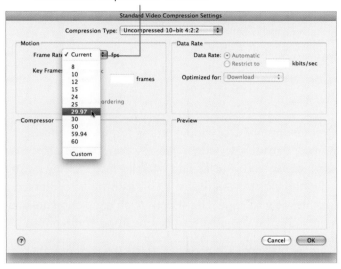

NOTE ▶ If you are using Apple ProRes, make sure to enable the Interlaced option and set the proper output field order.

In the Frame Controls pane, set the correct output field order: Top first or Bottom first. Typically HD video is Top field and SD NTSC video is Bottom field.

In the Frame Controls pane, set the retiming options to govern the conversion between the source and the output frame rate. See "Retiming Controls" in this lesson for information on the retiming controls.

Retiming Controls

When changes in frame rate are introduced into a conversion—such as in converting 29.97 fps NTSC to 25 fps PAL—the retiming controls can be used to increase the output quality significantly.

Rate Conversion pop-up menu

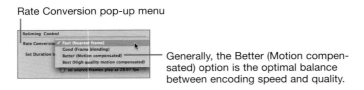

Generally, the Better (Motion compensated) option is the optimal balance between encoding speed and quality.

Quality vs. Encoding Time	Rate Conversion Choice
Fastest encoding	Fast (Nearest frame). Depending on the format conversion, Compressor removes or adds frames by copying the neighboring frames on either side. This setting will introduce choppy playback (frame judder) except when used with mostly static content, such as interview footage. Use it only when encoding speed is paramount and the source media can bear the compromise.
Good quality with average faster conversion time	Good (Frame blending). Compressor blends the picture data of neighboring frames to smooth the removal of frames or to cover the addition of frames to the frame-rate conversion.
Better quality with slower conversion time	Better (Motion compensated). Compressor uses optical flow to determine the vector path of each pixel from frame to frame and completely reinterprets the source media in the new frame rate.
Best quality	Best (High quality motion compensated). This setting increases the detail value of the optical flow motion calculations, placing each pixel more precisely in the reconstructed frame rate. Consider this option only when you are increasing the frame rate (adding frames). The significant increase in encoding time is not offset by greater quality when you use this option for frame-rate reductions.

Retiming Audio

In all instances, when audio accompanies video in source media, it will be retimed to match the new frame rate (or speed) of the output video. This ensures that the output audio and video remain in sync. Compressor will also pitch correct the audio so that it sounds the same as the original soundtrack.

QuickTime container-based targets allow you to "Pass-through" the audio in the Encoder settings.

Make sure to choose Enabled for all audio that you want synchronized with video during a retiming conversion.

Speed Changes

By default, the "Set Duration to" field in the retiming controls is set to 100.000% of source. With that setting, no changes in speed will occur even if the frame rate changes from one rate to another—for example, 29.97 fps NTSC to 25 fps PAL.

> **NOTE** ▶ When applying speed changes to media that contains audio, or audio-only media, the pitch will not shift because Compressor will automatically use Mac OS X's Core Audio technology during the conversion.

You can use Frame Controls in one of three ways to make constant speed changes to the output media:

By default, "Set Duration to" is set to 100% of source.

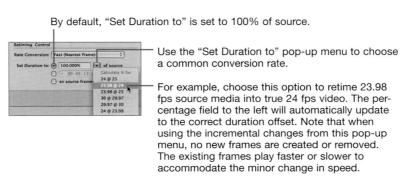

Use the "Set Duration to" pop-up menu to choose a common conversion rate.

For example, choose this option to retime 23.98 fps source media into true 24 fps video. The percentage field to the left will automatically update to the correct duration offset. Note that when using the incremental changes from this pop-up menu, no new frames are created or removed. The existing frames play faster or slower to accommodate the minor change in speed.

You can input a custom percentage directly in the "Set Duration to" field. Values greater than 100.000% will cause the output content to slow down, and values less than 100.000% will speed up the output. This behavior is the opposite of Final Cut Pro's Speed Tools in which lower percentages slow down clips and higher percentages speed up clips.

Using timecode to determine the speed change is very similar to a fit to fill edit in Final Cut Pro, whereby you set an edit duration and the source clip either speeds up or slows down to fill into the edit.

The percentage field automatically updates to the correct duration offset.

Select the radio button next to the timecode field and enter a new duration into the field. When you hold the pointer over the individual hours, minutes, seconds, and frames values, up and down triangles appear above and below the field. You can drag the up and down arrows to move the values forward or backward.

Selecting the last "Set Duration to" option is similar to the way Cinema Tools retimes media by conforming the source frame rate into the target frame rate. With this option selected, Compressor will not employ optical flow in the conversion.

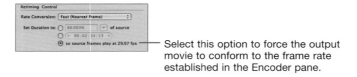

Select this option to force the output movie to conform to the frame rate established in the Encoder pane.

TIP ▶ It's common to have a video or audio clip that is a few seconds (or frames) too long or too short. You can use the retiming controls to fit the output clip exactly into your time constraints. You can use Apple's Motion or the Speed Tools in Final Cut Pro to create variable speed changes.

Frame Controls in the Real World

The results of settings made in the Frame Controls pane do not appear in the Preview window, so a real-time preview of their impact is not available. However, because of the potentially lengthy encoding times when frame controls are applied, you will want to use a test-clip workflow (see Lesson 5) on small sections of the source media to audition the settings. This carries a twofold benefit: You will not waste time encoding the entire media with an unsatisfactory setting, and you can estimate encoding times for the entire media based on the test times. For example, if one minute of footage is encoded in five minutes, it will take roughly five hours to encode one hour of footage with the same settings.

To evaluate your understanding of the concepts covered in this lesson and to prepare for the Apple Pro Certification Exam, download the online quiz at www.peachpit.com/apts.compressor.

Core Concepts

- Apply additive filters
- Apply corrective filters
- Apply color filters

Lesson 7
Customizing with Filters

Filters allow you to add audiovisual elements to your output media, such as watermarks and timecode burns, audio fade-ins and fade-outs, color adjustments, and many other general modifications. Filters are applied during encoding as separate tasks, apart from the target's codec, and you can apply a single filter or multiple filters to each target.

Applying Filters

Compressor includes a series of video, audio, and color filters you can combine with Apple and custom settings to modify the look of encoded media. You can preview the filter results in real time in the Preview window (see Lesson 5).

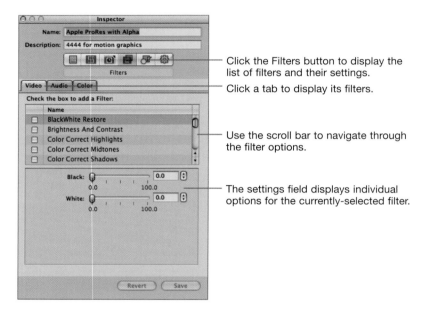

Click the Filters button to display the list of filters and their settings.

Click a tab to display its filters.

Use the scroll bar to navigate through the filter options.

The settings field displays individual options for the currently-selected filter.

Audio and Video filters are applied in the same manner, but the Color filter is applied to the entire job as a single setting. Compressor's Help documentation describes each filter in detail, but here is an introduction to some commonly used filters:

Applying Additive Filters

Several filter options add image elements to the data stream during encoding. For example, reference timecode is often added to video during post-production. You can easily add a timecode display during encoding using the Timecode Generator filter.

Enable a filter by selecting its corresponding checkbox.

By default, the Timecode Generator filter uses the source clip's timecode. You can override this default and start the timecode at zero by selecting the "Start Timecode at 00:00:00:00" option.

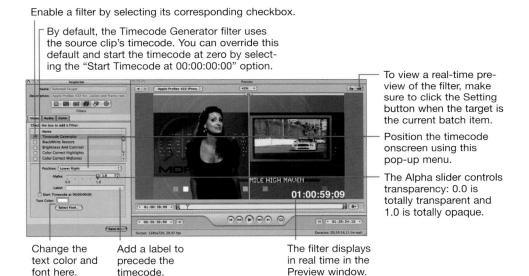

To view a real-time preview of the filter, make sure to click the Setting button when the target is the current batch item.

Position the timecode onscreen using this pop-up menu.

The Alpha slider controls transparency: 0.0 is totally transparent and 1.0 is totally opaque.

Change the text color and font here.

Add a label to precede the timecode.

The filter displays in real time in the Preview window.

Opening the Preview window during filter adjustment makes the process easier because you can see changes update in real time.

Other additive filters are applied in a similar fashion. For example, you could use the Watermark or Text Overlay filter to add a company logo or copyright notice to the video. In most cases, you'll need to define what is added, where to add it, and its appearance.

The Fade In/Out filters in both the Video and Audio tabs are additive filters that create stand-alone clips by adjusting the opacity of the picture and gain of the sound.

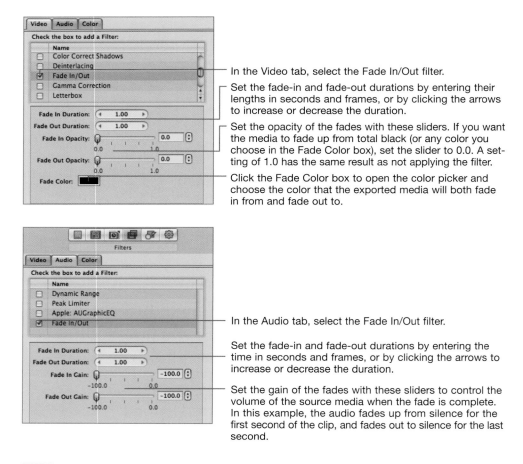

In the Video tab, select the Fade In/Out filter.

Set the fade-in and fade-out durations by entering their lengths in seconds and frames, or by clicking the arrows to increase or decrease the duration.

Set the opacity of the fades with these sliders. If you want the media to fade up from total black (or any color you choose in the Fade Color box), set the slider to 0.0. A setting of 1.0 has the same result as not applying the filter.

Click the Fade Color box to open the color picker and choose the color that the exported media will both fade in from and fade out to.

In the Audio tab, select the Fade In/Out filter.

Set the fade-in and fade-out durations by entering the time in seconds and frames, or by clicking the arrows to increase or decrease the duration.

Set the gain of the fades with these sliders to control the volume of the source media when the fade is complete. In this example, the audio fades up from silence for the first second of the clip, and fades out to silence for the last second.

TIP You can set In and Out points in the Preview window (see Lesson 1) and then use the Fade In/Out filters to make a subclip from your source media that fades the audio and video at the beginning and end of the output movie.

Applying a Corrective Filter

Like content filters, corrective filters can adjust specific visual aspects of the output media. When encoding a low-bandwidth job for the web, for example, you may find that the resulting image appears too soft. A Sharpen Edge filter can counteract an apparent loss of detail caused by the encoding process.

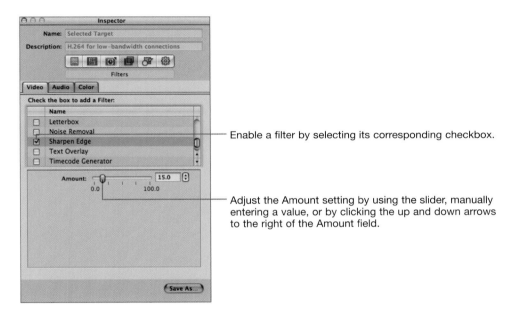

Enable a filter by selecting its corresponding checkbox.

Adjust the Amount setting by using the slider, manually entering a value, or by clicking the up and down arrows to the right of the Amount field.

When using the Sharpen Edge filter or any of the corrective filters, ease into the adjustment. For the most part, a little of each filter goes a long way. For example, setting the Sharpen Edge filter to a value greater than 25 can create fairly severe looking video (although that may be the creative look you are trying to achieve). Corrective filters can be used both artistically and aesthetically to manipulate the output image; similar to the way color correction, for instance, can play both an objective role (achieving optimal color values) and an artistic role (establishing a unique appearance for a scene).

TIP ▶ You'll notice some redundancy between a few of the filters and the Frame Controls options. For example, in addition to a Deinterlace filter, you have access to Deinterlace options in the Frame Controls pane of the Inspector; you have a Letterbox filter, as well as the Padding setting in Frame Controls. As a general rule, Frame Controls will produce better quality but at the cost of longer encode times. Filters can provide you with more control over the effect; for example, you can change the color of the Letterbox filter, but you cannot change the color using the Padding controls. Try experimenting with the different looks you can achieve by using the techniques discussed in Lesson 5.

Applying Color Filters

Compressor supports multiple output color spaces: YUV, 2YUV, RGBA, ARGB, and YUV (210). For each target output, Compressor chooses the optimal color space based on quality and encoding performance. Certain codecs and codec/filter combinations may change Compressor's default choice for a given job. In the Color tab, you can choose from the Output Color Space pop-up menu to override Compressor's default assignment for the output media.

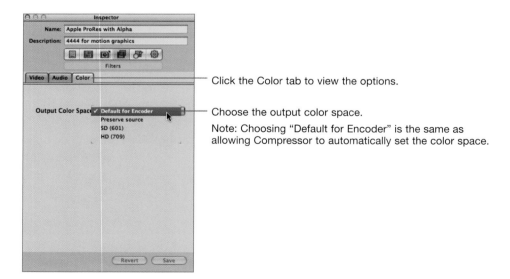

Click the Color tab to view the options.

Choose the output color space.

Note: Choosing "Default for Encoder" is the same as allowing Compressor to automatically set the color space.

If you are not satisfied with the output color space of a given encode, try setting the output color space to Preserve Source. With that setting chosen, Compressor will attempt to maintain the source media color space through the encoding process. If the output media is bound for broadcast television or optical disc delivery, selecting the SD or HD options may provide better output color fidelity for those distribution platforms.

> **NOTE ▸** Certain codecs—MPEG-2, for example—have fixed color spaces and, as a result, the Output Color Space pop-up menu will be dimmed and unavailable.

Setting Render Order

Filters are always rendered in top-down list order. Although Compressor initially lists filters alphabetically, you can change the rendering order by dragging and rearranging filters in the list. This is useful when you want to change the render order of multiple activated filters. For example, if you place a Timecode Generator followed by a Letterbox filter, you may obscure your timecode with the letterbox. By swapping the order of the filters in the list to render the Letterbox filter first, you can help ensure that your timecode will be seen.

To evaluate your understanding of the concepts covered in this lesson and to prepare for the Apple Pro Certification Exam, download the online quiz at www.peachpit.com/apts.compressor.

8
Core Concepts

Lesson 8
Transforming with Geometry Settings

While you'll use the Inspector's Encoder and Frame Controls pane for the "heavy lifting" in Compressor, in the other panes you'll fine-tune and finesse encoding jobs. In the Geometry pane, you'll change the output frame size, adjust the aspect ratio of the output movie, and pad the source movie inside the output frame size.

Using the Geometry Pane

Although aesthetic or logistical considerations are key when choosing frame dimensions, scaling down to a smaller output frame size is a common strategy for reducing overall file size. For example, an HD movie with a 1280 x 720 pixel frame size can be reduced to a 640 x 360 frame, creating a smaller file that is acceptable for computer playback. This size reduction has a direct correlation to a decrease in output file size; smaller frame sizes require less data.

In some instances, Compressor will dictate the output frame size and dim the options in the Geometry pane. The SD DVD specification, for example, requires a fixed frame size of 720 x 480 pixels. Therefore, the Geometry options are dimmed and unavailable for all DVD settings, including HD to SD downcoverts.

Click the Geometry button to open the Geometry pane.

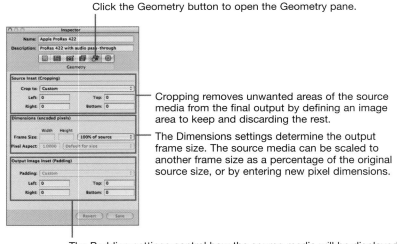

Cropping removes unwanted areas of the source media from the final output by defining an image area to keep and discarding the rest.

The Dimensions settings determine the output frame size. The source media can be scaled to another frame size as a percentage of the original source size, or by entering new pixel dimensions.

The Padding settings control how the source media will be displayed within the frame size established by the Dimensions controls.

Changing Frame Dimensions

Use the Dimensions (encoded pixels) controls to transform the source media's frame width, height, and aspect ratio to different values.

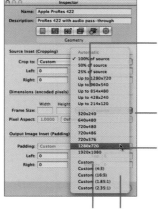

The percentage options change the output frame size based on an exact percentage of the source media size. The "Up to" options will maintain the source media's native aspect ratio while transforming the frame size up to the selected dimensions.

Note: The final output will not exceed the source's native dimensions or the selected dimension. Therefore, do not use these options for upscaling. Instead, choose a specific frame size or enter custom values in the Width and Height fields.

Click the Frame Size pop-up menu to define the output dimensions.

The fixed frame size options set output dimensions to the values in the list. If you choose a frame size with an aspect ratio that's different from your source, the source media will be scaled during encoding.

The Custom option displays whenever you input values directly into the Frame Size Width and Height fields.

The Custom options with common aspect ratios affect only the source's Height value. For example, if 320 x 240 is the current frame size and you choose Custom (16:9), Compressor will adjust the Height to 180 and leave the Width unchanged.

Click the Pixel Aspect pop-up menu to force the output media's pixels into one of the listed aspect ratios. Choosing "Default for size" will leave the source media's aspect ratio unchanged. When encoding media intended for playback on computer displays, choose Square.

Tip: The DVCPRO HD and HDV options will help you set the correct aspect ratio for HD formats that employ anamorphic frame sizes to achieve true 1920 x 1080 or 1280 x 720 HD video.

Cropping Media

By default, Compressor uses the entire source media frame during the encoding process. You can redefine which part of the image will be encoded by creating a source inset.

Compressor offers two ways to crop media: a visual method using the Preview window, and a numerical method using the Geometry pane.

To crop using the Preview window, select a target in the Batch window or click the Batch Item pop-up menu and choose a target.

Drag the Split Screen slider to the left to see the entire cropped image.

If you cannot see the cropping boundaries, make sure that the Preview window's display is relative to the source media (not the output) and that the preset (not the source) is loaded into the Preview screen area.

Red cropping boundaries surround the source media. You can adjust all four sides of the image by dragging those boundaries to define the part of the image to be encoded.

While dragging a boundary, Compressor displays the numeric values of the crop.

You can drag the sides of the cropping boundaries independently, or constrain the entire crop to the aspect ratio of the source media by holding down Shift while dragging one of the corner handles. The cropping boundaries' values will update automatically in the Geometry pane. You can also reposition the entire box by clicking in the center of the box and dragging it to a new location.

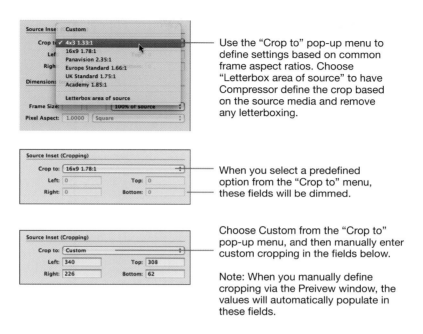

Use the "Crop to" pop-up menu to define settings based on common frame aspect ratios. Choose "Letterbox area of source" to have Compressor define the crop based on the source media and remove any letterboxing.

When you select a predefined option from the "Crop to" menu, these fields will be dimmed.

Choose Custom from the "Crop to" pop-up menu, and then manually enter custom cropping in the fields below.

Note: When you manually define cropping via the Preivew window, the values will automatically populate in these fields.

The Source Inset (Cropping) controls work in tandem with the Dimensions (encoded pixels) controls. For example, if you crop a movie and have a fixed output dimension, the cropped source media will be scaled to fit inside the fixed-frame dimensions.

To apply a crop and not scale the output media, in the Frame Size pop-up menu, choose 100% of Source, or manually enter the frame-size values based on the resulting reduction of the crop. For example, if a 720 x 480 frame was cropped 40 lines from the top and 40 lines from the bottom, enter a custom frame size of 720 x 400.

Padding the Output

If cropping limits which part of the visual image Compressor will encode, then padding dictates which part of the output frame the source media will occupy. For instance, if you have a DV NTSC clip that's 720 x 480 and you apply an HD frame size (1280 x 720) target, by default, the DV source clip will be scaled up to fill the entire frame size. Using padding, you can maintain the DV's actual 4:3 aspect ratio and play it *within* the output HD (16:9) frame size of 1280 x 720.

The following example uses the Padding controls to retain a SD, 4:3 aspect ratio within the HD output dimensions.

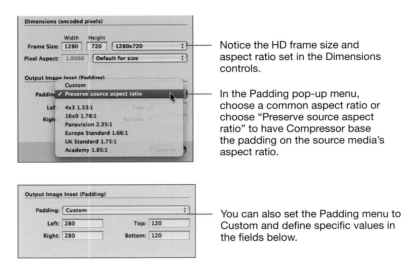

Notice the HD frame size and aspect ratio set in the Dimensions controls.

In the Padding pop-up menu, choose a common aspect ratio or choose "Preserve source aspect ratio" to have Compressor base the padding on the source media's aspect ratio.

You can also set the Padding menu to Custom and define specific values in the fields below.

TIP Select the source media's job in the Batch window to view its dimensions and aspect ratio in the Inspector window

Padding, in essence, creates a matte around the source media inside the output frame size, much as you would frame a painting or photograph post. This can be used in several practical and creative situations. For example, a network might want you to deliver a full HD-framed movie of standard definition source media. You could use padding to have your SD content play back in its original frame size and aspect ratio within a 16:9 HD frame. The black, empty areas of the border could later be filled with commercial content from the network or additional content of your own (think of Bloomberg Television).

Another example would occur in a post-production workflow where you are building elements for HD delivery and are responsible for only one element in the frame. You could inset your content into the frame and leave the rest of the frame available for others.

TIP ▶ The Apple ProRes codecs are good choices for this type of work.

Exploring the Math Behind the Numbers

All the functions in the Geometry pane can significantly alter the presentation of your output video, so it is essential to understand why certain values produce certain results. For example, if you start with HD source media at 1920 x 1080 and choose the MPEG-4, 300Kbps Apple setting, the default output frame size will be 320 x 240. Houston, we have a problem! Compressor will do exactly what you tell it to do: It will squeeze the 16:9 footage into a 4:3 box and your movie will look like the opening sequence of Kung-Fu Theatre—the image is pushed in at the sides making everything look tall and thin.

Video frame sizes ranging from web delivery to SD to HD are all governed by width and height proportions called aspect ratios. For example, DV NTSC has a frame size of 720 pixels wide by 480 pixels high (720 x 480). The aspect ratio for that frame size is 3:2, meaning that for every 3 pixels in width, the image is 2 pixels tall. That's why, when you look at a DV NTSC image, it's not a square, it's a rectangle.

The following table lists basic calculations for the most common frame sizes. You can use this information in the Geometry pane to correct display problems in your output movies and also to creatively produce unconventional frame sizes.

Using the table, you can quickly deduce the proper frame size if you have just one of the output dimensions. For example, a common task is creating web-ready versions of 16:9 movies. The common 320 x 240 web output frame size represents a 4:3 aspect ratio. It will not accurately display 16:9 content because the source is scaled to fit (which changes the aspect ratio). But, using the 16:9 calculation in the table, you can derive the proper widescreen height for a 320-pixel width by multiplying 320 by .5625, which equals 180 pixels. Granted, Compressor addresses this common output issue in the Dimensions settings where you can easily set the widescreen aspect using the pop-up menus, but the calculations listed in the following table can address any custom situation you may encounter.

NOTE ▶ When setting custom frame dimensions, it's best to set the Pixel Aspect to Square to avoid any unwanted distortion of the output movies during playback.

Frame Size	Aspect Ratio	Width Calculation	Height Calculation
DV NTSC 720 x 480	3:2	Multiply the height by 1.5	Multiply the width by .667
Widescreen DV 720 x 480 (squeezed)	16:9	Multiply the height by 1.778	Multiply the width by .5625
HD 1280 x 720	16:9	Multiply the height by 1.778	Multiply the width by .5625
HD 1920 x 1080	16:9	Multiply the height by 1.778	Multiply the width by .5625
HDV 1440 x 1080	16:9	Multiply the height by 1.333	Multiply the width by .75
Web 320 x 240	4:3	Multiply the height by 1.333	Multiply the width by .75
N/A	Academy 1:85:1	Multiply the height by 1.851	Multiply the width by .5403
N/A	Panavision 2:35:1	Multiply the height by 2.351	Multiply the width by .425

NOTE ▶ Some equations may not produce whole numbers. Screen dimensions cannot include fractions, so you must round off fractional values. For example, if the height equals 319.23, round up the height value to 320 pixels.

To evaluate your understanding of the concepts covered in this lesson and to prepare for the Apple Pro Certification Exam, download the online quiz at www.peachpit.com/apts.compressor.

9

Core Concepts

Control efficiency and quality in Final Cut Studio with Apple ProRes codecs

Create format conversions

Work with image sequences

Create surround sound assets

Work with markers to enhance encoding and navigation

Annotate media with metadata

Work with closed captions

Lesson **9**

Advanced Output

Although Droplets and batch templates make Compressor an efficient tool for day-to-day post-production needs, it is also a robust application for the compressionist who requires the highest level of control over the encoding process.

Compressor contains advanced features that allow for very specific or highly specialized output. You may not need these tools often, but having them available makes Compressor as deep as it is wide.

Working with Apple ProRes

Production codecs create files in an intermediate format that let you retain quality while conforming digital assets to a post-production standard. In a file-based workflow, production codecs perform the same function that dub masters perform in a tape-based workflow.

The five versions of Apple ProRes included with Final Cut Studio provide a versatile set of production codec options specifically designed and tuned for Final Cut Studio and Apple hardware.

The Apple ProRes family maintains the source frame size and frame rate and employs a highly efficient variable bit rate encoder. The set of Apple ProRes codecs cover a range of delivery bandwidths while simultaneously retaining high image fidelity while reducing overall system demands compared to other production codecs, such as 10-bit uncompressed or Photo-JPEG, or camera codecs such as DVCPro HD or HDV. The following table illustrates how each of the Apple ProRes versions targets a specific quality, bandwidth and performance demographic:

	Apple ProRes 4444	Apple ProRes 422 (HQ)	Apple ProRes 422	Apple ProRes 422 (LT)	Apple ProRes (Proxy)
Target data rate for HD 1080i	330 Mbps	220 Mbps	147 Mbps	102 Mbps	45 Mbps
Target data rate for HD 720p	132 Mbps	88 Mbps	59 Mbps	41 Mbps	18 Mbps
Target data rate for NTSC SD	94 Mbps	63 Mbps	42 Mbps	29 Mbps	12 Mbps
Simultaneous streams of HD 1080p content on a Mac Pro (8-core, 2.93 GHz)	5	10	13	16	21

	Apple ProRes 4444	Apple ProRes 422 (HQ)	Apple ProRes 422	Apple ProRes 422 (LT)	Apple ProRes (Proxy)
Simultaneous streams of HD 1080p content on a MacBook Pro (17 inch, 2.8 GHz Core 2 Duo)	n/a	2	3	4	5

Here are some suggested uses for each Apple ProRes version:

▶ Apple ProRes 4444: Mastering content for online workflows and high-end acquisition formats such as RED ONE, HDCAM SR, and Thomson Viper. Also motion graphics work that requires an alpha channel.

▶ Apple ProRes 422 (HQ): Transcode HDV, AVCHD, and AVC-Intra for increased quality and performance in Final Cut Studio. Highest quality in the 4:2:2 color space. Also good for graphics and gradients in the 4:2:2 colorspace without an alpha channel.

▶ Apple ProRes 422: Lower bandwidth version of the ProRes 422 codec when compared to (HQ). Requires fewer resources than (HQ), good for reducing ingest and media storage overhead with minimal loss in quality.

▶ Apple ProRes 422 (LT): Good for news, sports, and live-broadcast programming. Thirty percent less overhead than Apple ProRes 422. Upsample 4:1:1 and 4:2:0 color spaces to 4:2:2 without significant increase in storage and bandwidth overhead.

▶ Apple ProRes (Proxy): Up to 70% less bandwidth than Apple ProRes 422. Full raster frame sizes for offline editorial with significant real-time capabilities, even on portable systems. Final Cut Server proxy media.

Compressor includes multiple Apple ProRes settings contained within various groups in the Settings window. You can use Compressor's search function in the Settings window to easily locate individual Apple ProRes versions.

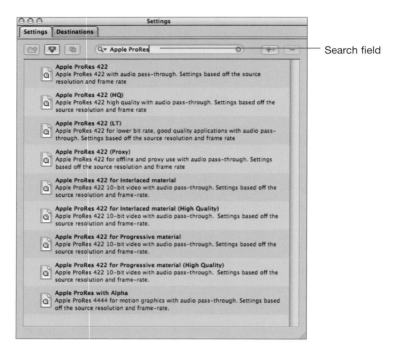

When selecting Apple ProRes 422 settings, base your choice on the desired output quality (see the previous table) and whether you need interlaced or progressive video. For example, if you want to transcode camera-native progressive HD footage into the highest quality 4:2:2 color space format, you could apply the "Apple ProRes 422 for Progressive material (High Quality)" setting to all the footage. This would retain overall picture quality, frame size, and frame rate; it also creates media requiring significantly less processor overhead than the camera-native format when editing in Final Cut Pro.

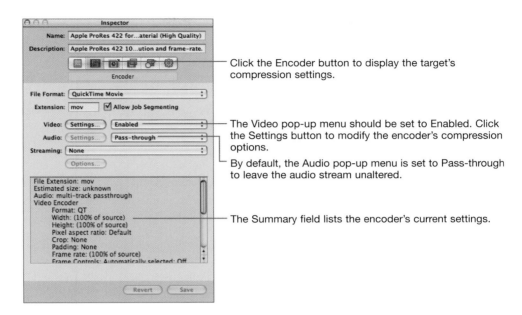

Click the Encoder button to display the target's compression settings.

The Video pop-up menu should be set to Enabled. Click the Settings button to modify the encoder's compression options.

By default, the Audio pop-up menu is set to Pass-through to leave the audio stream unaltered.

The Summary field lists the encoder's current settings.

When you click the Settings button next to the Video pop-up menu, the QuickTime Compression Settings window opens.

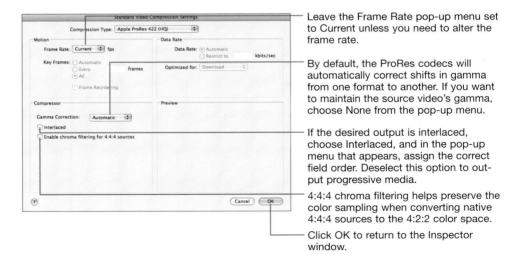

Leave the Frame Rate pop-up menu set to Current unless you need to alter the frame rate.

By default, the ProRes codecs will automatically correct shifts in gamma from one format to another. If you want to maintain the source video's gamma, choose None from the pop-up menu.

If the desired output is interlaced, choose Interlaced, and in the pop-up menu that appears, assign the correct field order. Deselect this option to output progressive media.

4:4:4 chroma filtering helps preserve the color sampling when converting native 4:4:4 sources to the 4:2:2 color space.

Click OK to return to the Inspector window.

> **TIP** ▶ Because the data rate and the balance of the encoding parameters are set automatically by the individual Apple ProRes codecs, all ProRes versions are similarly configured.

In addition to standardizing media within Final Cut Studio workflows, the Apple ProRes family works very well within Compressor as intermediate transcoders during job chains (see Lesson 3). Apple ProRes 4444 and Apple ProRes 422 (HQ) are especially suitable for this task.

> **TIP** ▶ The Apple ProRes 4444 codec contains a high-quality alpha channel and, since it's tuned for Final Cut Studio, should be used for motion graphics work instead of the Animation codec. The default export format from Motion is Apple ProRes 4444.

Easy Export, found in the Share menus of both Final Cut Pro and Motion, also offers streamlined access to the Apple ProRes codecs.

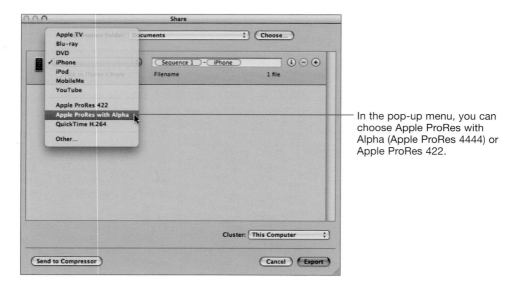

In the pop-up menu, you can choose Apple ProRes with Alpha (Apple ProRes 4444) or Apple ProRes 422.

> **NOTE** ▶ Compressor also includes settings for the Apple Intermediate Codec (AIC). This codec is used primarily for transcoding Long-GOP HDV footage into an all I-frame video stream that provides better overall system performance when editing with Final Cut Express or iMovie.

Creating Format Conversions

Format conversions (also known as standards conversions) are the result of transcoding source media from one format into another format.

A golden rule of transcoding is: To achieve the highest quality output media, you should start with source media of a quality equal to or higher than your desired output. For example, you will produce significantly better format conversions when transcoding from HD to SD, from larger frames to smaller frames (such as 1280 x 720 to 320 x 180), and from uncompressed to compressed formats (such as 10-bit to DV) than when transcoding any of those examples in reverse.

Performing HD to SD Downconversions

Material shot in any HD format (including HDV) has stunning quality compared to SD formats. However, HD material is often downconverted to lower resolution (and smaller file size) formats such as standard-definition DVDs and iPhone- or iPod-compatible movies. Compressor can process the downconversion from HD to a smaller format while simultaneously encoding the output media.

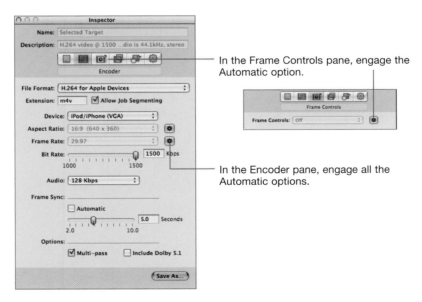

In the Frame Controls pane, engage the Automatic option.

In the Encoder pane, engage all the Automatic options.

In this example, HD source media is being encoded and downconverted for playback on an iPhone or iPod.

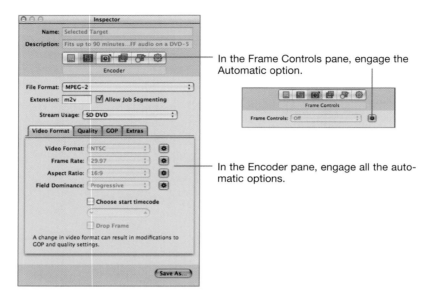

In the Frame Controls pane, engage the Automatic option.

In the Encoder pane, engage all the automatic options.

In this example, HD source media is being encoded and downconverted into an MPEG-2 elementary stream for use in SD DVD authoring.

NOTE ▶ You can engage the automatic Frame Controls option only when performing HD downconversions similar to the two examples just shown. For all other conversions, you will need to manually set Frame Controls (see Lesson 6).

In general, HD material takes longer to compress than SD material when going to a standard-definition output (such as SD DVD), because, in addition to applying the encoding settings, Compressor also conforms the frame size of the HD source media to the smaller frame size of the output format.

TIP ▶ In the preceding examples, downconversion and encoding were performed simultaneously. You can control the render order of the downconversion using the job chaining techniques described in Lesson 3.

Applying Other Format Conversions

In addition to downconverting HD material to SD DVDs and Apple mobile devices, Compressor offers several presets that convert HD source media to SD media, and vice versa, using QuickTime container files.

Compressor also produces high-quality cross-conversions. For example, NTSC and PAL are SD formats that differ in frame rate and frame size. Converting from one standard to the other requires both retiming and reframing—two operations that benefit greatly from the optical flow technology contained within Compressor's Frame Controls (see Lesson 6).

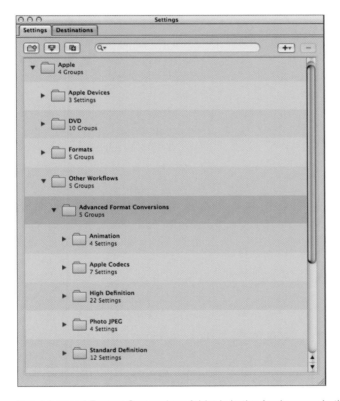

The Advanced Format Conversions folder is in the Apple group in the Other Workflows path.

The following table describes each of the settings contained in the five Advanced Format Conversions groups:

Group	Setting	Use
Animation	Animation NTSC, PAL	Lossless, high-quality codec used in CGI, motion graphics, titles, and so on. Includes workflows in both the NTSC and PAL frame sizes and rates.
Animation	Animation NTSC, PAL (Alpha)	Adds an alpha channel for transparency.
Apple Codecs	AIC and Apple ProRes 422	Refer to the sections in this Lesson that cover these production codecs.
High Definition	DVCPro HD: 1080i/50, 1080i/60, 720p/24, and 720p/60	Panasonic high-definition codec. Choose a setting based on the output frame size and frame rate. For example, choose the DVCPro HD 720p/24 setting to output a 1280 x 720 movie with 24 progressive frames per second, compressed using the DVCPro HD codec.
High Definition	HD uncompressed 10-bit: 1080i/50, 1080i/60, and 1080p/24	Uncompressed high-definition codec using 10-bit video. Choose a setting based on output frame size and rate.
High Definition	HD uncompressed 8-bit: 1080i/50, 1080i/60, and 1080p/24	Uncompressed high-definition codec using 8-bit video. Choose a setting based on output frame size and rate.
High Definition	HDV: 1080i/50, 1080i/60, 720p/30	High-definition codec that uses Long GOP MPEG-2 compression. Used in Sony and JVC video cameras. Choose a setting based on frame size and output hardware compatibility.
High Definition	XDCAM HD	Long-GOP MPEG-2 Compression from Sony (also known as MPEG HD) in 1080i and 1080p formats.

Group	Setting	Use
Photo JPEG	JPEG 100 NTSC, PAL	High-quality, intraframe compression codec used in post-production. Choose a setting based on output format: NTSC or PAL.
Photo JPEG	PEG 75 NTSC, PAL	Good quality with smaller output file sizes than JPEG 100. Choose a setting based on output format: NTSC or PAL.
Standard Definition	DV NTSC, PAL	Common production and post-production codec that provides good quality with low resource overhead. Choose a setting based on output format: NTSC or PAL.
Standard Definition	DV NTSC, PAL (Anamorphic)	Widescreen (16:9) version of the settings.
Standard Definition	DVCPro 50 NTSC, PAL	Panasonic codec with video quality similar to DigiBeta and double the file size and resource requirements of DV. Choose a setting based on output format: NTSC or PAL.
Standard Definition	DVCPro 50 NTSC, PAL (Anamorphic)	Widescreen (16:9) version of the settings.
Standard Definition	SD 10-bit Uncompressed NTSC, PAL	High-quality post-production codec commonly used to digitize analog sources and as a common editorial format. Choose a setting based on output format: NTSC or PAL.
Standard Definition	SD 8-bit Uncompressed NTSC, PAL	Codec that balances good video quality with lower resource requirements than 10-bit. Choose a setting based on output format: NTSC or PAL.

All of the Advanced Format Conversion settings are modified in QuickTime Video Compression Settings windows via the Inspector.

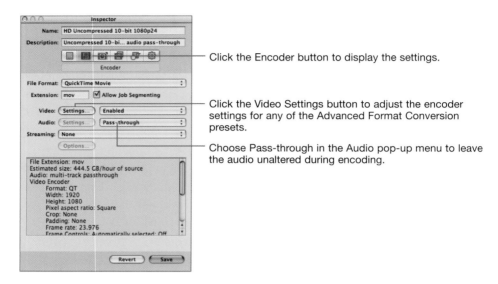

Click the Encoder button to display the settings.

Click the Video Settings button to adjust the encoder settings for any of the Advanced Format Conversion presets.

Choose Pass-through in the Audio pop-up menu to leave the audio unaltered during encoding.

The QuickTime Video Compression Settings window contains all of the codec settings for the Advanced Format Conversion presets. The window is divided into four sections: Motion, Data Rate, Compressor, and Preview.

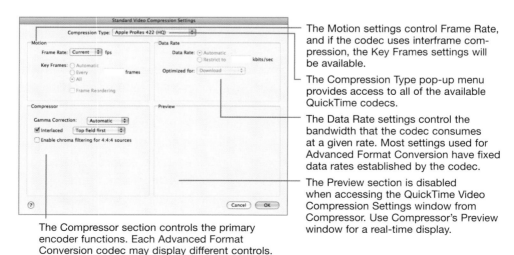

The Motion settings control Frame Rate, and if the codec uses interframe compression, the Key Frames settings will be available.

The Compression Type pop-up menu provides access to all of the available QuickTime codecs.

The Data Rate settings control the bandwidth that the codec consumes at a given rate. Most settings used for Advanced Format Conversion have fixed data rates established by the codec.

The Preview section is disabled when accessing the QuickTime Video Compression Settings window from Compressor. Use Compressor's Preview window for a real-time display.

The Compressor section controls the primary encoder functions. Each Advanced Format Conversion codec may display different controls.

TIP ▶ Any format or standards conversion that includes a change in frame rate, frame size, or both—such as transcoding from NTSC to PAL—will benefit from Compressor's Frame Controls (see Lesson 6).

In the Settings window within the various Apple setting groups, you will find that some codecs are repeated and some settings overlap. For example, the Apple > Other Workflows > Motion Graphics folder contains many of the same settings as the Advanced Format Conversions folder. Compressor provides multiple paths to the same settings that will ultimately produce the same results.

Although each folder may contain settings found in other folders, it may also contain unique settings. For instance, the Motion Graphics folder contains two unique Pixlet settings, in addition to several settings also found in the Advanced Format Conversions folder. The Pixlet codec is used almost exclusively by animators and motion graphic artists as a production codec and is of little use elsewhere.

TIP ▶ To find the best advanced setting for a particular target output, start by entering a combination of codec and format keywords in the Settings window's search field.

Working with Image Sequences

In addition to transcoding video from one format to another, you can also use Compressor to create still images from motion video and vice versa. When working on effects shots or complex composites, you may need to convert media into a series of individual frames, known as an *image sequence*. Conversely, you may receive a folder of still images—DPX files, for example—that must be converted to a QuickTime movie for editing in Final Cut Pro.

Creating Image Sequences

Compressor does not contain an Apple setting for creating image sequences, so you'll have to create a custom setting for this purpose.

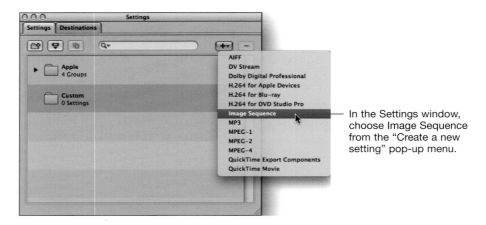

In the Settings window, choose Image Sequence from the "Create a new setting" pop-up menu.

A new custom setting will appear in the Custom folder. Select it to open it in the Inspector.

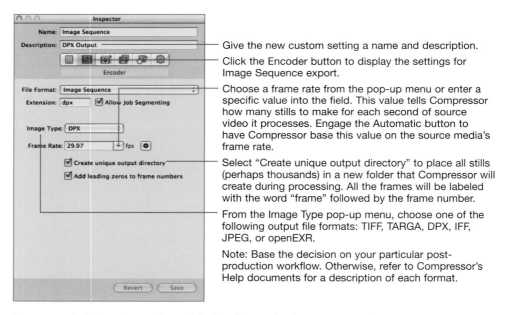

Give the new custom setting a name and description.

Click the Encoder button to display the settings for Image Sequence export.

Choose a frame rate from the pop-up menu or enter a specific value into the field. This value tells Compressor how many stills to make for each second of source video it processes. Engage the Automatic button to have Compressor base this value on the source media's frame rate.

Select "Create unique output directory" to place all stills (perhaps thousands) in a new folder that Compressor will create during processing. All the frames will be labeled with the word "frame" followed by the frame number.

From the Image Type pop-up menu, choose one of the following output file formats: TIFF, TARGA, DPX, IFF, JPEG, or openEXR.

Note: Base the decision on your particular post-production workflow. Otherwise, refer to Compressor's Help documents for a description of each format.

You can apply this custom setting to jobs just like any Apple or custom setting.

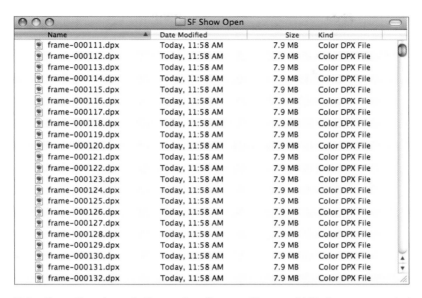

Using the setting shown in the previous figure, a 15-second HD clip was converted into a sequence of 500 still images.

NOTE ▶ The output image files will have the same frame size as the source media. So, if the source media is HD 1080p, the resulting image files will have a pixel resolution of 1920 x 1080.

Importing Image Sequences

You can import a folder of still images into Compressor and output them as a single, stand-alone QuickTime movie.

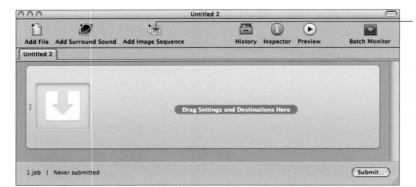

Click the Add Image Sequence button. When the Open dialog appears, navigate to the folder that contains the sequence of images and click Open.

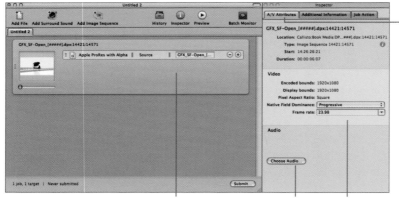

With the job selected in the Batch window, click the A/V Attributes tab to set the parameters of the imported image sequence.

Add a QuickTime target to the image sequence job in the Batch window.

Tip: Apple ProRes 4444 or Apple ProRes 422 (HQ) are each good formats for high-resolution image sequences. Refer to "Working with Apple ProRes" in this lesson for more information.

You can marry an audio file to the image sequence and Compressor will treat them as a single source. Click Choose Audio and then select the file from the Open dialog.

The frame size and pixel aspect ratio are defined by the images, but you can use the corresponding menus to interpret both the field dominance (interlaced or progressive) and the frame rate.

Tip: Confer with the author of the image sequence for the proper frame rate. Interpreting the image sequence incorrectly may result in any output movie playing at the wrong speed.

After image sequences have been imported and interpreted, you can treat them just like any other job, that is, you can add a target and then submit the batch.

Creating Surround Sound Assets

Creating a surround sound mix is a five-step process, but Compressor is involved in only the final two steps:

1. Record audio on a sound stage or in a recording studio.

2. Mix down the audio into separate audio channels that locate the sounds in surround space. You can use Soundtrack Pro to create a surround sound mix.

3. Export the audio into 48 kHz audio files (in AIFF, QuickTime, or WAV format).

4. Identify the channel placement.

5. Encode the source media into a single AC3 or QuickTime file that's targeted for the specific delivery platform (DVD, BD, broadcast, and so on).

The first three steps require a considerable amount of hardware and software, but after the resulting source media files are created, you can use Compressor to produce surround sound AC3 media or a QuickTime surround sound file.

Click the Add Surround Sound button.

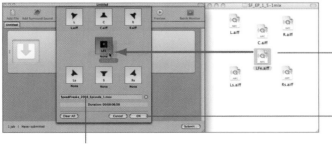

Drag the source sound files from the Finder to the corresponding channel in the channel assignment interface.

When all the channels are assigned, click OK. Compressor will place a single entry in the Batch table comprising all the input channels.

You can marry a video file to the surround sound job and Compressor will treat them as a single source. Click Add Video and then select the file from the Open dialog.

Compressor will display the video's name and duration. To remove the video, click the "x" button.

TIP ▶ As another method, click the channel icons in the channel assignment interface, and then choose the source media from the dialogs that appear.

If you need to edit the channels, select the surround sound entry in the Batch window to open the channel assignment interface in the Inspector. Perform any changes and then click Save.

If you've added a video file to the job, you can export a stand-alone QuickTime movie—such as Apple ProRes 422 (HQ)—or export audio and video elementary streams for optical disc delivery (DVD or Blu-ray Disc).

Click the Audio Settings button to assign the proper
QuickTime channel assignments.

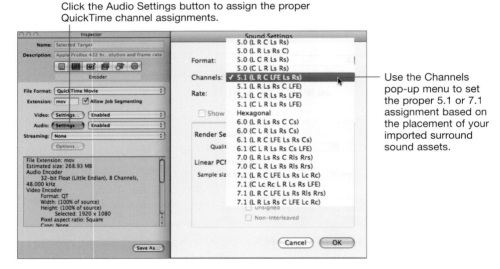

Use the Channels pop-up menu to set the proper 5.1 or 7.1 assignment based on the placement of your imported surround sound assets.

In this example an Apple ProRes 422 (HQ) target was added to a surround sound job that contained a video asset.

If only audio assets were added to the job, you can export either Dolby Digital Professional or QuickTime Surround 5.1 assets.

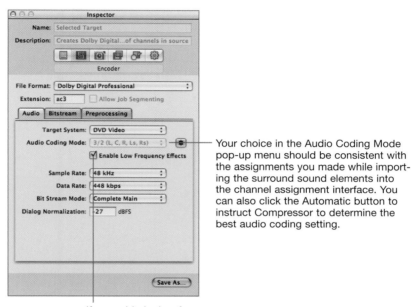

Your choice in the Audio Coding Mode pop-up menu should be consistent with the assignments you made while importing the surround sound elements into the channel assignment interface. You can also click the Automatic button to instruct Compressor to determine the best audio coding setting.

If you added a low frequency effects (LFE) channel in your assignments, be sure to select the Enable Low Frequency Effects checkbox.

In this example a Dolby Digital Professional (Auto) target was added to a surround sound job.

After all of the assignments and modifications are complete, click the Submit button in the Batch window.

NOTE ► You can submit Dolby Digital Professional 2.0 jobs by assigning the left and right channels manually and then adding a Dolby Digital Professional 2.0 target.

Auditioning AC3 Assets

You can preview Dolby Digital Professional encoded files (AC3) within Compressor before you send the assets to a DVD-authoring platform such as DVD Studio Pro. Additionally, because Compressor treats the Dolby-encoded stream as it would any other imported audio asset, you can transcode the AC3 files into another audio format.

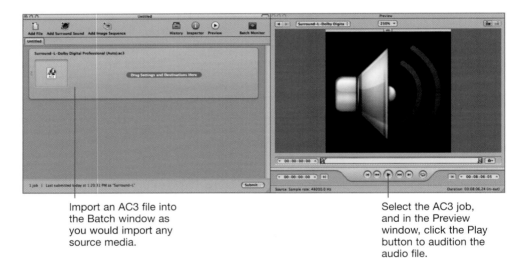

Import an AC3 file into the Batch window as you would import any source media.

Select the AC3 job, and in the Preview window, click the Play button to audition the audio file.

NOTE ► If you do not have a 5.1 sound system connected to your computer, Compressor will downmix the audio to Dolby 2.0 (stereo) during playback.

Working with Markers

Compressor provides four types of markers in two basic categories: compression and navigation. Compression markers help the encoding engine more effectively process the output media by defining areas of focus, such as an area of extreme motion. Navigation markers add metadata to the output media that enhances the viewer's experience with the content, such as chapter markers on a DVD.

> **NOTE** ▶ Only the following output formats support markers: MPEG-2, MPEG-4 (when properly configured for podcasting), QuickTime movies, and H.264 for Apple devices and DVD Studio Pro.

Regardless of how individual markers are defined, you initially add markers in the same way:

1. Create a new job and import source media (see Lesson 3).
2. Load the job into the Preview window (see Lesson 1).
3. Place the playhead on the desired frame (see Lesson 1).
4. Press M.

Viewing Edit/Cut Markers

Final Cut Pro places a compression marker at every cut point in a sequence. Cuts or edits can often signify an abrupt change in the visual landscape of the movie—for example, when cutting from a dark room to a sunny beach. Marking those areas aids compression by telling the encoder that the transition between frames might be abrupt and could require more attention and more video data during encoding compared to frames that remain constant.

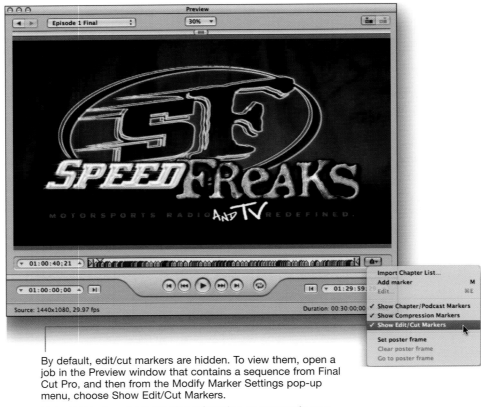

By default, edit/cut markers are hidden. To view them, open a job in the Preview window that contains a sequence from Final Cut Pro, and then from the Modify Marker Settings pop-up menu, choose Show Edit/Cut Markers.

Note: Edit/cut markers are also referred to as automatic compression markers, and they are colored green in the Preview window.

Creating Compression Markers

Compressor also lets you add manual compression markers to the source media. Compression markers force an I-frame at the marker location during encoding and can be useful when encoding quick camera movements or fast, onscreen motion because they force the encoder to add more video data to that section.

Move the play-
head to the
desired frame
and press M
to place a
compression
marker.

Note:
Compression
markers are
colored blue
in the Preview
window.

Alternatively, from the Modify
Marker Settings pop-up menu,
choose "Add marker."

TIP ▶ Use compression markers sparingly and place them only on the most chal-
lenging parts of your source media. Applying too many compression markers will
clog the encoder with I-frames and defeat the overall purpose of compression.

You can view the marker's settings by positioning the playhead directly on the marker and
pressing Command-E.

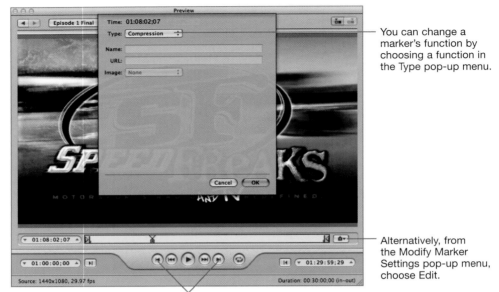

You can change a marker's function by choosing a function in the Type pop-up menu.

Alternatively, from the Modify Marker Settings pop-up menu, choose Edit.

Click the "Move to Previous Marker" and "Move to Next Marker" buttons to easily navigate between markers in the Preview window's timeline.

Note: The playhead must be placed exactly on a marker to modify the marker.

Delete compression markers by placing the playhead on the marker and pressing M, or from the Modify Marker Settings pop-up menu, choosing "Remove marker."

Creating Chapter Markers

You can create chapter markers directly in Compressor that will appear in DVD Studio Pro. Chapter markers will also appear within QuickTime Player when displaying a compatible movie.

> **NOTE ▶** Chapter markers applied to source media in Final Cut Pro will automatically appear in Compressor's Preview window.

In the Preview window, navigate to the desired frame, press M, and then press Command-E to edit the marker.

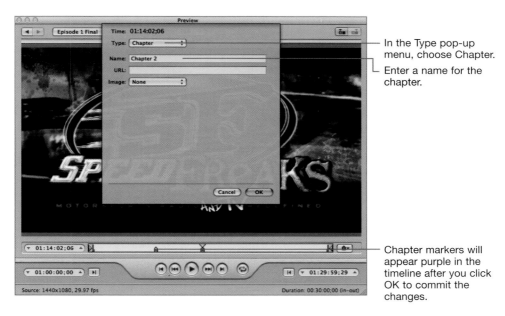

In the Type pop-up menu, choose Chapter.

Enter a name for the chapter.

Chapter markers will appear purple in the timeline after you click OK to commit the changes.

Delete chapter markers by placing the playhead on the marker and pressing M, or from the Modify Marker Settings pop-up menu, choosing "Remove marker."

TIP ▸ You can use chapter markers in QuickTime movies during post-production to aid the collaborative process. For example, you could create a movie that contains markers that let the production team navigate quickly and easily to the different sections of the show.

Adding URL Podcast Markers

You can place markers in the video stream that will enable interactivity in Compressor's output files. For example, you can add an HTML link that will appear onscreen at a designated time and take the viewer to a website when clicked (if the client computer is connected to the Internet).

In the Preview window, navigate to the desired frame, press M, and then press Command-E to edit the marker.

> **TIP** You can also use podcast markers to add image data to an audio-only podcast. From the Image pop-up menu, choose a still image that you want to appear in the data stream. Next, apply one of the audio podcasting settings in Apple > Other Workflows > Podcasting and submit the batch for encoding. The image markers will appear when the podcast is played in an application such as iTunes or on Apple Devices, such as iPods, iPhones, and Apple TVs.

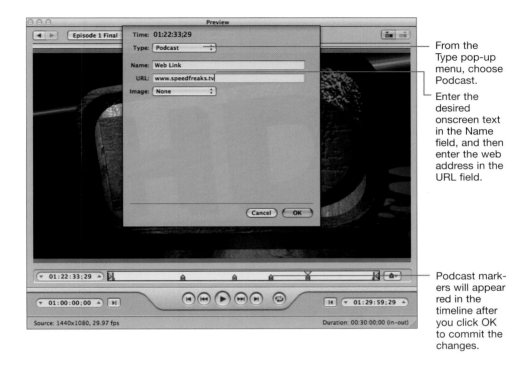

From the Type pop-up menu, choose Podcast.

Enter the desired onscreen text in the Name field, and then enter the web address in the URL field.

Podcast markers will appear red in the timeline after you click OK to commit the changes.

Annotating Media with Metadata

You can add metadata, such as a copyright notice or author information, to your source media. The metadata is embedded in the output file during encoding. This information will not be visible in the video stream, but it can be accessed when a viewer chooses Get Info in applications such as QuickTime Player or iTunes.

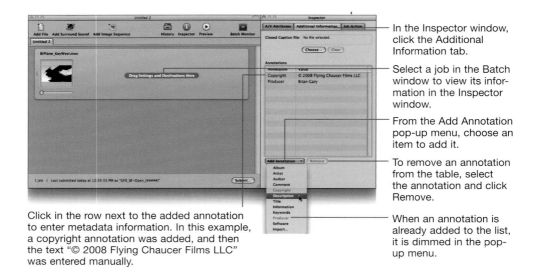

In the Inspector window, click the Additional Information tab.

Select a job in the Batch window to view its information in the Inspector window.

From the Add Annotation pop-up menu, choose an item to add it.

To remove an annotation from the table, select the annotation and click Remove.

When an annotation is already added to the list, it is dimmed in the pop-up menu.

Click in the row next to the added annotation to enter metadata information. In this example, a copyright annotation was added, and then the text "© 2008 Flying Chaucer Films LLC" was entered manually.

NOTE ▶ Annotations are supported by the following output formats: H.264 for Apple devices, MP3, and QuickTime movie.

Working with Closed Captions

You can use Compressor to associate a closed caption file to a job that contains video source media.

NOTE ▶ A third-party service or software is required to create closed captions.

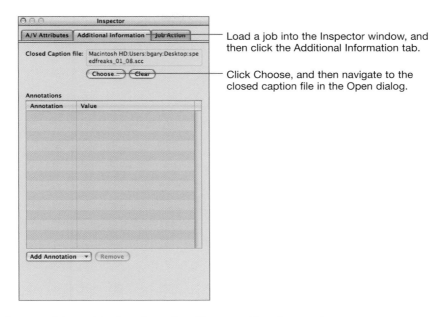

Load a job into the Inspector window, and then click the Additional Information tab.

Click Choose, and then navigate to the closed caption file in the Open dialog.

When working with closed caption files, consider these points:

▶ The timecode of the closed caption file must relate exactly to the source media's time-code, otherwise the captions may not be in sync with the onscreen video.

▶ The closed caption file must be in the Scenarist Closed Caption (.scc) format.

▶ Closed caption data is supported only by the following formats: MPEG-2, QuickTime movie, and H.264 for Apple devices.

▶ When working with output from QuickTime movies and H.264 for Apple devices, the closed captions are included as a separate track in the container. QuickTime Player 7.2 and higher can display closed captions.

▶ Compressor embeds the closed captions into the video stream during MPEG-2 exports. DVD Studio Pro retains the information when authoring SD NTSC projects.

To evaluate your understanding of the concepts covered in this lesson and to prepare for the Apple Pro Certification Exam, download the online quiz at www.peachpit.com/apts.compressor.

10

Core Concepts

Three basic rules of compression

Encoding tips and techniques

Lesson 10
Compressionist's Cheat Sheet

Compressor is to encoding what Final Cut Pro is to editing, meaning that the underlying skills are learned separately from the software used to perform them. While Compressor makes encoding accessible to all, behind its interface lies intense codec engineering and mathematics that generally fall into a "dark arts" category where few tread and even fewer seek any level of mastery. Although you can produce excellent results by mastering Compressor as an application, a deeper understanding of compression technology and technique is essential to becoming an encoding expert.

Although encoding can be a very exacting craft, it's also an art form governed by aesthetics. Compression exists for the purpose of delivering digital media in a cost-effective manner, but it also has to *look* and *sound* good, and that is the marriage of the science and the art.

When videotape was the primary delivery format for completed content, the online media was often a lateral digital copy of the tape. For example, 10-bit uncompressed video was ingested from DigiBeta tapes, and then the final edit was laid back to DigiBeta with very little quality loss.

Today's reality is that the final delivery format is very often a compressed version of the online master. HDCAM SR and D-5 tapes still provide very high-quality HD masters with minimal degradation from the source. But if your final content is intended for an optical medium such as Blu-ray Disc or DVD, or broadcast distribution via transport and program streams, or mobile devices and the Web, then the final version of your content will be a highly compressed version of the original. The goal is to produce a compressed version of your content that's *visually lossless* when compared to the original.

Three Basic Rules of Compression

The mathematics governing compression may be quite complex and complicated, but the basic rules governing their use are quite simple and easy to follow.

Start with the Highest Quality Source Media

The highest quality media can usually be defined as the media that is closest to the production media or the online masters. For example, if you have an Apple ProRes 422 (HQ) file and a DVD of your movie and want to encode a version for the web, choosing the ProRes file will produce significantly higher-quality encodes because of its greater resolution and video fidelity. Remember, just because the DVD was the "final" version of the project doesn't mean that it's the best encoding source.

Compare Encoded Media Only to the Source, Not Other Encodes

When following the test clip workflows in Lesson 5, it's tempting to compare the various test encodes in hopes of finding a "winner." Your goal, though, is finding the output settings that produce the most visually lossless media within the particular delivery constraints. Therefore, comparing the encoded media to the source is the only way to accurately judge the results of compression.

Compression Requires Compromise

The well-worn project triangle of "fast, cheap, and good" says that you can realize two qualities from the list, but that you never can achieve all three. The underlying message of compromise translates perfectly to encoding, and in many ways it's just an either/or choice. For example, you can have either high quality or small file size, fast encoding or multi-pass encoding, increased file compatibility or increased file functionality. Your goal always should be to clearly define your compromises so that you can best inform your encoding decisions.

Core Concepts and Tips

Compressor's batch templates (Lesson 2) remove many of the technical barriers of digital distribution because after you tell it what you want Compressor performs all the heavy lifting. Moving from the batch templates to Compressor's intermediate and advanced workflows requires some basic understanding of compression technology.

Every Source Is Unique

It's tempting to seek out a one-size-fits-all approach to encoding. Granted, Droplets and templates appear to provide that solution, but in reality they are one-size-fits-most applications. The first step in becoming a compressionist is realizing that every project and every source media clip has unique properties and idiosyncrasies.

Identifying the following items in your source media will inform your evaluation of the project by focusing your attention on those elements that are the greatest encoding challenges:

▶ Rapid camera movements (swishes, pans, crash zooms, and so on)

▶ Fast movement within the shot or many objects moving simultaneously within the shot

▶ Night scenes or scenes shot with low available light

▶ Scenes with wide dynamic range: the brightest whites to the darkest blacks

> **TIP** ▶ Find any of these sections in your source media and then use the test clip workflows described in Lesson 5 to encode just those portions. If you can achieve good results with those most challenging sections, the same settings will produce good results with the balance of the source media.

Find the "Impact Player"

Just as in professional sports, in which a single player can have a disproportionate effect on the outcome of the game, a single compression setting can have a disproportionate effect on the quality of the encoded output. A perfect example of a Compressor "impact player" is bit rate, or data rate.

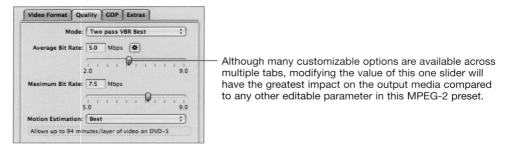

Although many customizable options are available across multiple tabs, modifying the value of this one slider will have the greatest impact on the output media compared to any other editable parameter in this MPEG-2 preset.

MPEG-2 setting in the Encoder pane of the Inspector window

When working with bit rates or data rates, you will have to choose a compromise between file size and media quality. The more bits, or data, that you apply to the encode, the greater the visual (and/or audio) quality, but at the expense of increased file size.

> **TIP** The megabit and the megabyte (10 Mbps versus 10 MBps, for example) are two units of measurement that are often confused, especially when referring to data throughput. Megabits (Mbps) measure data transfer; megabytes (MBps) measure data storage (file size). The confusion arises because both are also used to describe bandwidth and throughput in the same way that inches and centimeters describe distance. The conversion between the two is 1 Mbps = 0.125 MBps, or more precisely 8 bits = 1 byte.

Intraframe vs. Interframe Compression

When applying intraframe compression, every frame of video exists individually, and any data reduction (encoding) that is achieved resides within the boundaries of each frame. It is often referred to as *all I-frame video.*

In contrast, interframe compression removes large groups of whole frames and replaces them with algorithmic data sequences that a playback device (iPod, DVD, QuickTime Player) decodes and interprets as video. From a production, post-production, and digital distribution standpoint, the difference between these two methods is enormous. Understanding when to use each one is an essential skill.

Because intraframe compression includes a frame of video for every frame captured, it's often used in camera acquisition and post-production editorial in these common formats: DV NTSC, DVCPro HD, Apple ProRes (all versions), and 10-bit uncompressed. The actual compression that occurs within each frame can vary greatly among the formats, but every frame will exist at the given frame rate. The cost of all this data is large file sizes when compared to content encoded with interframe compression. The overall picture fidelity and editorial ease in applications such as Final Cut Pro make intraframe compression a good choice for streamlined post-production.

Interframe compression employs temporal encoding that places code and algorithms between full video frames in the data stream. The interstitial math determines the differences between those full frames, and during playback it resolves how to represent that interpretation as video. Removing the vast majority of full frames results in a significant reduction in overall file size, but at the expense of quality when compared to content encoded with intraframe compression. Delivery formats such as DVD (MPEG-2) and Blu-ray Disc (AVC) use interframe encoding exclusively to produce widely distributable media in the most cost-effective manner. Therefore, apply interframe compression (H.264 and MPEG-2, for example) when delivering your content to final distribution formats such as YouTube, MobileMe, iPhones and iPods, DVDs, and Blu-ray Discs.

> **TIP** ▶ Some consumer and prosumer camera platforms such as HDV and AVC-Intra employ interframe compression to allow high definition acquisition to tape and solid-state media such as compact flash cards, but you may find that transcoding that material into an intraframe format produces a better post-production workflow. Refer to the "Working with Apple ProRes" section in Lesson 9 for more information on transcoding into a production codec.

To evaluate your understanding of the concepts covered in this lesson and to prepare for the Apple Pro Certification Exam, download the online quiz at www.peachpit.com/apts.compressor.

11

Core Concepts

Enhance Compressor with QuickTime components and plug-ins

Use the command line for highly advanced Compressor workflows

Lesson 11
Expanding Compressor

Compressor installs with a series of settings that represent a wide range of deliverable media, but you can also tweak and customize those settings to produce an even greater array of content.

Additionally, Compressor supports third-party components and plug-ins that allow it to expand beyond the default QuickTime codecs and settings. So, you can increase your range of delivery formats while maintaining your current Compressor digital distribution workflow.

Before installing any third-party elements into Final Cut Studio, always ensure that the incoming software is compatible with your current versions of Final Cut Studio (including all individual dot releases), Mac OS X, and QuickTime. Also, be sure to follow each manufacturer's installation procedures for any hardware or software components.

Using QuickTime Components

QuickTime components offer a streamlined approach to a specific delivery format. For example, Telestream's Flip4Mac WMV (www.telestream.net/flip4mac-wmv/overview.htm) software lets you encode directly to the Windows Media format within Compressor.

> **NOTE ▶** QuickTime components do not utilize all facets of the Compressor workflow: namely, Frame Controls or the Geometry settings. Therefore, you must set all of the output parameters in the component's custom interface.

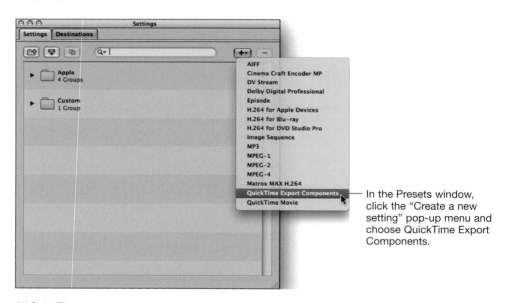

In the Presets window, click the "Create a new setting" pop-up menu and choose QuickTime Export Components.

All QuickTime components require you to create a new custom setting.

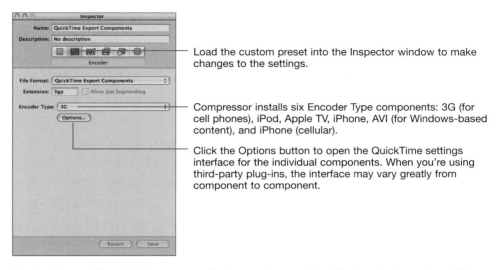

Load the custom preset into the Inspector window to make changes to the settings.

Compressor installs six Encoder Type components: 3G (for cell phones), iPod, Apple TV, iPhone, AVI (for Windows-based content), and iPhone (cellular).

Click the Options button to open the QuickTime settings interface for the individual components. When you're using third-party plug-ins, the interface may vary greatly from component to component.

Use the Save and Revert buttons to respectively commit or cancel modifications to the custom setting.

The Flip4Mac WMV codec will appear in the Inspector window in the Encoder Type pop-up menu as "Windows Media." Clicking the Options button provides access to all the Flip4Mac WMV settings via a QuickTime window.

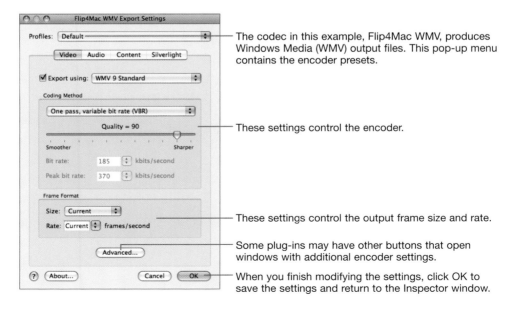

The codec in this example, Flip4Mac WMV, produces Windows Media (WMV) output files. This pop-up menu contains the encoder presets.

These settings control the encoder.

These settings control the output frame size and rate.

Some plug-ins may have other buttons that open windows with additional encoder settings.

When you finish modifying the settings, click OK to save the settings and return to the Inspector window.

Apply QuickTime component settings just as you would apply any other setting to a job in the Batch window.

> **NOTE** ▶ QuickTime component settings may create files that encode correctly for the target platform but do not play in QuickTime Player.

Consult the Compressor support web pages (www.apple.com/support/compressor) to verify the compatibility of third-party software.

Using Compressor Plug-ins

Plug-ins differ from QuickTime components in two key ways:

▶ They utilize the entire Compressor workflow (Frame Controls, Geometry settings, and so on). In essence, they function like the default Apple settings.

▶ They install custom settings or their own options in the "Create a new setting" pop-up menu in the Settings window.

Encoding with Cinema Craft Encoder MP

The Compressor plug-in from Cinema Craft, CCE-MP (http://omni-cinemacraft.com), produces high-quality MPEG-2 elementary video streams for DVD.

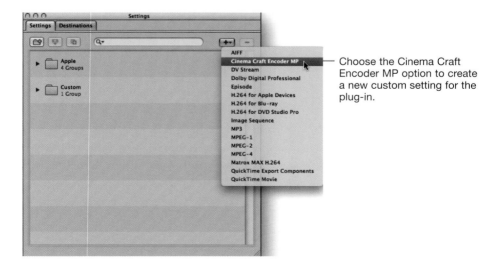

Choose the Cinema Craft Encoder MP option to create a new custom setting for the plug-in.

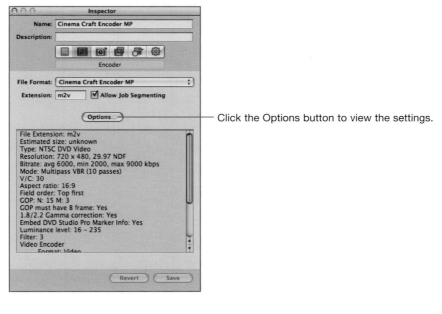

Click the Options button to view the settings.

After you click the Options button, a Templates window appears in which you can narrow down your encoding settings based on your source media.

In this example, NTSC video will be encoded for DVD.

Click OK to commit the template.

NOTE ▶ Choosing Other in the center column will allow you to create High level MPEG-2 video streams with data rates up to 40 Mbps. These streams can be used for some broadcast platforms and also Blu-ray Discs. Be aware, though, that the DVD spec supports main level streams only up to 9.8 Mbps.

Clicking Options again in the Inspector opens the detailed settings for the custom CCE-MP preset.

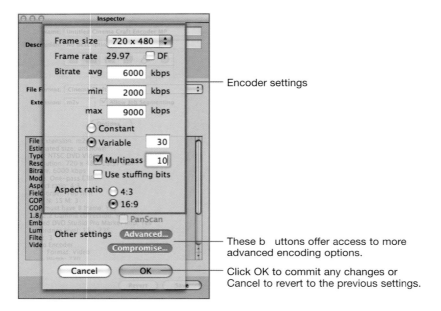

Refer to the CCE-MP documentation for specific instructions on the use of the plug-in.

TIP When downconverting HD source material for SD DVD delivery, make sure to engage Frame Controls (see Lesson 6) when encoding with CCE-MP.

Compressing with Episode Encoder

Telestream's Episode Encoder (www.telestream.net/episode/overview.htm) works with a wide range of codecs such as Flash, VC1, and Windows Media.

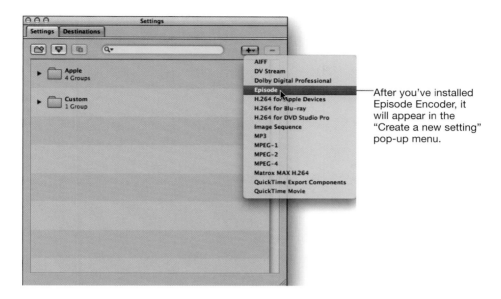

After you've installed Episode Encoder, it will appear in the "Create a new setting" pop-up menu.

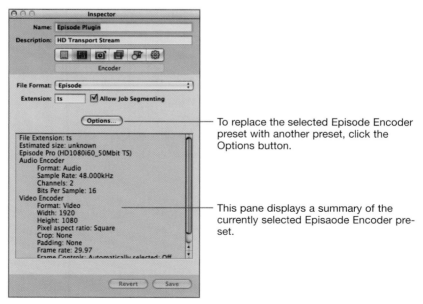

To replace the selected Episode Encoder preset with another preset, click the Options button.

This pane displays a summary of the currently selected Episaode Encoder preset.

After you click Options, the following drop-down window appears:

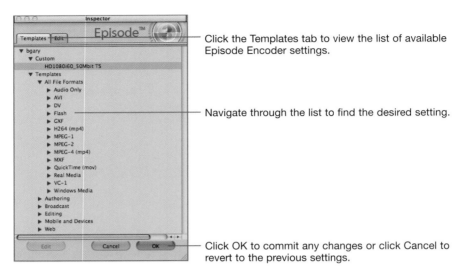

Click the Templates tab to view the list of available Episode Encoder settings.

Navigate through the list to find the desired setting.

Click OK to commit any changes or click Cancel to revert to the previous settings.

Only the Windows Media and Flash presets can be edited using the Edit tab, or by clicking the Edit button. (For all other presets, the Edit button will remain dimmed.) You will need to use Episode Encoder itself to modify the rest of the presets in the list.

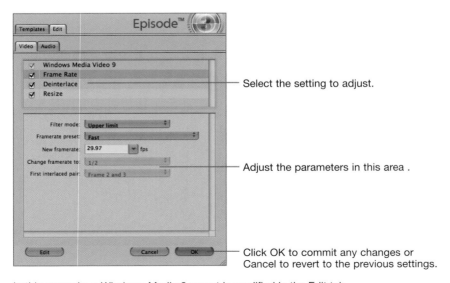

Select the setting to adjust.

Adjust the parameters in this area .

Click OK to commit any changes or Cancel to revert to the previous settings.

In this example, a Windows Media 9 preset is modified in the Edit tab.

You can add custom Episode Encoder settings to jobs in the Batch window just as you can add any Apple or custom setting.

> **NOTE ▶** To create custom Episode Encoder presets, you will need to work within Episode Encoder; but once created, the presets will appear in the Compressor plug-in interface.

Encoding with Matrox CompressHD

The Matrox CompressHD system uses both hardware acceleration and a software plug-in to encode H.264 (AVC) for Blu-ray Discs, the Web, and mobile devices. Follow the manufacturer's instructions for installing the PCI card (Mac Pro only) and the software.

The CompressHD system installs both custom settings and a custom option in the "Create a new setting" pop-up menu.

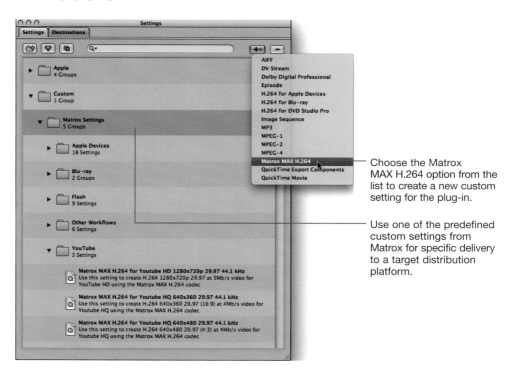

Choose the Matrox MAX H.264 option from the list to create a new custom setting for the plug-in.

Use one of the predefined custom settings from Matrox for specific delivery to a target distribution platform.

Depending on the type of Matrox plug-in preset you select in the Settings window,
Compressor will display one of two types of presets in the Inspector window:

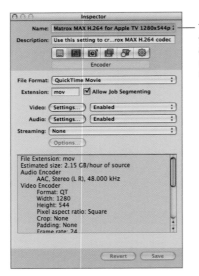

This QuickTime container preset uses
the Matrox Max H.264 codec (via the PCI
card) to produce stand-alone QuickTime
movies for playback on the Web or
mobile devices.

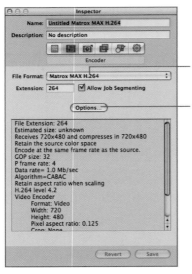

This type of Matrox preset uses the Matrox Max H.264
codec (via the PCI card) to create elementary video streams
for Blu-ray Discs.

Click Options to open the settings window.

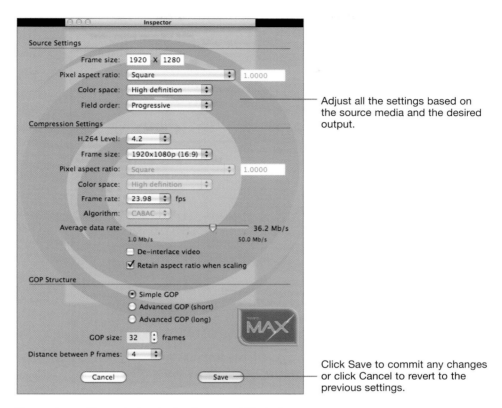

Adjust all the settings based on the source media and the desired output.

Click Save to commit any changes or click Cancel to revert to the previous settings.

The custom settings window for the CompressHD plugin.

MORE INFO ▶ Refer to the Matrox CompressHD documentation for specific instructions on the use of the plug-in and the hardware. For more information about the Matrox CompressHD system, visit www.matrox.com/video/en/products/compresshd.

Using Compressor in the Command Line

The Compressor application is the graphical user interface for *compressor*, the process that submits jobs to the Compressor transcoder and runs entirely in the background—that's why you can quit Compressor, but your batches will continue encoding. That also means you can interact with the compressor process directly from the command line (using Terminal) and submit batches to the Compressor transcoder without opening the Compressor application. Technically speaking, this technique may not be expanding Compressor, but it's definitely capable of expanding your use and understanding of Compressor as a whole.

Still, working with any application from the command line is not for the faint of heart. It is useful, however, for large volume encoding or for making Compressor part of a larger scripted operation. Controlling the compressor process via the command line in Terminal can be very powerful.

Compressor's Help documents include an appendix on the command line functions, but here's an overview:

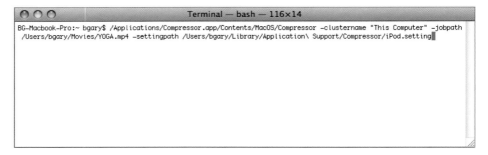

The default location for the Terminal application is the Utilities folder of the Applications folder on your hard drive.

The command in the Terminal window shown in the previous figure tells the compressor process to encode a specific file with a specific setting and submit it to the local computer for processing.

Here's how it breaks down:

/Applications/Compressor.app/Contents/MacOS/Compressor

This is the command that tells the computer what to do. In this case, it runs the Compressor command.

-clustername "This Computer"

The –clustername phrase is called an *argument*, another word for parameter, and the *subject* of this argument is "This Computer." Therefore, this parameter is telling the Compressor command to use the local machine (instead of a cluster) to encode the job.

-jobpath /Users/bgary/Movies/YOGA.mp4

The argument -jobpath defines the source movie, YOGA.mp4, which is the subject.

-settingpath /Users/bgary/Library/Application\ Support/Compressor/iPod.setting

The argument -settingpath, when used with the corresponding subject, tells Compressor what setting file to use. In this example, it uses a custom setting.

Pressing Return submits the job to the Compressor transcoder.

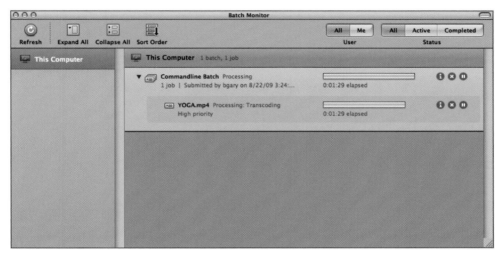

Batch submitted for encoding without opening the Compressor application.

Use the following command in the Terminal to view all the available options for running Compressor via the command line:

/Applications/Compressor.app/Contents/MacOS/Compressor –help

To evaluate your understanding of the concepts covered in this lesson and to prepare for the Apple Pro Certification Exam, download the online quiz at www.peachpit.com/apts.compressor.

12

Core Concepts

Install distributed processing in Final Cut Studio

Create QuickClusters (render farms) and virtual clusters

Distributed Processing

Distributed processing harnesses the collective encoding power of two or more computers on the same local area network (LAN)—sometimes referred to as a *render farm*. By spreading the encoding load across multiple computers, you can reduce processing time compared to using a single computer that's shouldering the entire job.

Before performing the tasks in this lesson, familiarize yourself with the Distributed Processing Setup Guide in Help > Compressor Help. You can also download the Apple Qmaster Distributed Processing Setup Guide.pdf from the Compressor Support section of Apple's website. Distributed processing works best with robust hardware environments in which the media is centralized on SANs (storage area networks) and connected to the Final Cut Studio workstations over a high-speed fiber channel network.

Installing Distributed Processing in Final Cut Studio

During the Final Cut Studio installation, the following screen appears that allows you to create an Apple Qmaster service node.

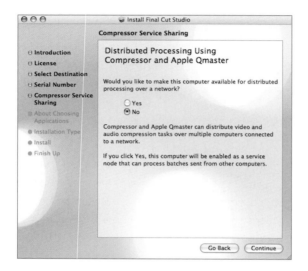

This window allows you to quickly set up distributed processing on the target computer by automatically designating it as an *unmanaged service node*—a computer available to encode network jobs. By default, the Compressor Service Sharing option is set to No. So, if you want the target computer to process batches on the network, select Yes, and then click Continue.

> **NOTE** ▶ Selecting Yes defines the following parameters: The target computer is shared as "Services Only;" the Compressor service is selected and unmanaged; and sharing is started automatically.

Creating a QuickCluster

Apple Qmaster, used in conjunction with Mac OS X and Compressor, allows you to create a simple, easily configured distributed processing network referred to as a QuickCluster. Before creating a network, consult the following table to verify that your hardware meets the minimum requirements:

Component	Hardware/Software Requirements
Network	All computers must be physically connected to a local network. (Gigabit Ethernet, Fiber Channel, and so on are suitable. Wireless connections are not recommended.)
	All computers must be on the same subnet of the local network.
Computer	All computers must be running the same version of Mac OS X, version 10.5.6 or higher.
	All computers must be running the same version of QuickTime, version 7.6 or higher.
	For optimal performance and compatibility, the same version of Final Cut Studio must be installed on each system to ensure that all Compressor settings are available to the QuickCluster. Non-matching configurations of Mac OS X, QuickTime, or Final Cut Studio are not supported.
	All computers must have read access to the source media and read/write access to the output destination.

Setting Up the Cluster Controller

You need to designate one computer as the cluster controller. This computer will send the encoding instructions with all the frames to the rest of the computers—the node computers—during processing.

On the computer designated as the cluster controller, click Apple Qmaster in System Preferences.

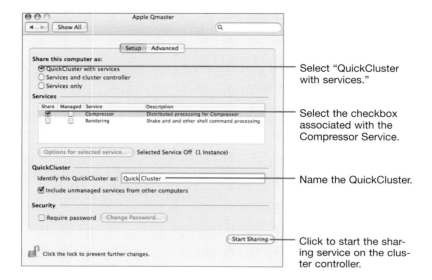

Select "QuickCluster with services."

Select the checkbox associated with the Compressor Service.

Name the QuickCluster.

Click to start the sharing service on the cluster controller.

NOTE ▶ Only one computer can be configured as the controller of the cluster, the rest of the computers must be configured as nodes.

Setting Up the Node Computer

If you selected Yes on the Distributed Processing Screen during the Final Cut Studio installation (see "Installing Distributed Processing in Final Cut Studio"), your computer will already be configured as an available node.

If you did not, you can easily configure your computer as a node by matching the following settings in Qmaster preferences:

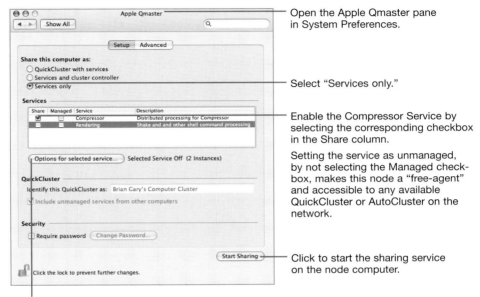

Open the Apple Qmaster pane in System Preferences.

Select "Services only."

Enable the Compressor Service by selecting the corresponding checkbox in the Share column.

Setting the service as unmanaged, by not selecting the Managed check-box, makes this node a "free-agent" and accessible to any available QuickCluster or AutoCluster on the network.

Click to start the sharing service on the node computer.

If your computer has multiple processors or multiple cores (instances), you can limit the number of resources that will be shared by clicking this button. (See the next figure for more details.)

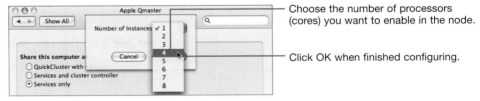

Choose the number of processors (cores) you want to enable in the node.

Click OK when finished configuring.

A drop-down window appears after clicking the "Options for selected service" button.

NOTE ▶ You might want to limit the available processors to retain computing power on your local computer. For example, you could make one processor in a computer available for distributed Compressor processes and leave the other processor available for local Final Cut Pro editing.

Qmaster can display the status of active services in the menu bar alongside the clock, AirPort status, Spotlight, and so on.

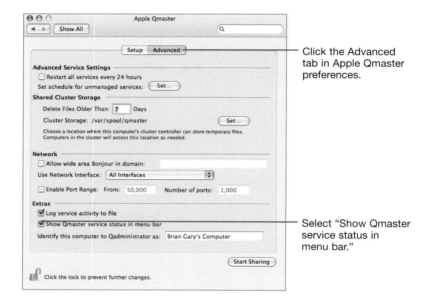

Click the Advanced tab in Apple Qmaster preferences.

Select "Show Qmaster service status in menu bar."

Submitting a Batch to a QuickCluster

You do not have to create a separate workflow for distributed processing. First, ensure that all targets in the batch are ready for distributed processing, and then click the Submit button in the Batch window.

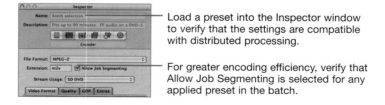

Load a preset into the Inspector window to verify that the settings are compatible with distributed processing.

For greater encoding efficiency, verify that Allow Job Segmenting is selected for any applied preset in the batch.

After clicking Submit in the Batch window, Compressor lets you decide where to send the batch for encoding.

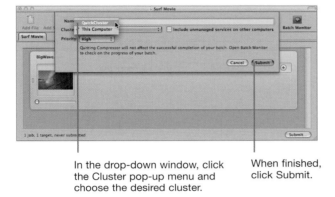

In the drop-down window, click the Cluster pop-up menu and choose the desired cluster.

When finished, click Submit.

Monitoring a QuickCluster

You can use the Batch Monitor to oversee encoding jobs on a QuickCluster, just as you monitor jobs processing on a local computer.

Choose your QuickCluster from the list in the left pane to display currently-encoding jobs in the right pane.

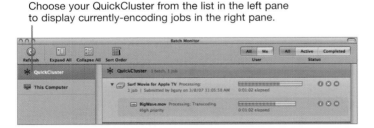

Troubleshooting QuickClusters

Distributed processing adds multiple variables to the encoding mix. Use the following table to troubleshoot some common issues:

Problem	Solution
Sequences exported directly from Final Cut Pro are not encoding in the QuickCluster.	When exporting sequences directly from Final Cut Pro to Compressor, you must install Final Cut Pro on each node computer for the QuickCluster to work properly. All the nodes must have access to the media referenced in the Final Cut Pro project—that is, the volume with the assets must be mounted on each computer. Note that every running network instance of Final Cut Pro must have a unique product serial number.
Node computers do not have access to some or all of the components of a QuickTime reference movie.	Use self-contained source media by having Final Cut Pro (or any other application creating the source media) write the entire contents of a movie to a single file, or consolidate the media on shared storage such as an Xsan.
Unsatisfactory quality issues arise from multi-pass encoding jobs sent to the QuickCluster.	Allowing Compressor to segment the job produces faster encoding times because different nodes are working concurrently on separate sections of the job. A potential problem arises with multi-pass presets. With unsegmented encoding, a single computer will analyze the whole media on the first pass to inform its compression decisions. When a job is segmented, each node reviews only a portion of the media on the first pass, so overall compression decisions are based only on that source segment. This may not produce the best results for source media that changes visual style considerably during its length—for example, a documentary that has static interviews and dynamic B-roll. Clearing the Allow Job Segmenting checkbox will output more consistent quality on multi-pass jobs, but will also reduce the overall distributed processing speed.

Creating Local Clusters

With any multiprocessor or multicore Mac, you can create a virtual cluster that treats each of your processors (or cores) as if it were a separate node computer. On a computer with robust resources, this can offer significant speed advantages during encoding, especially for codecs like H.264 that are not natively multi-threaded, because Qmaster will segment the job and send work to the separate processors as if they were different nodes on the network.

For example, if you want to encode a movie for iPhones (using, by default, the H.264 codec) and you submit the job to This Computer, the Compressor engine will only be able to harness one of your processors (cores) because H.264 is not multi-threaded. However, if you create a virtual cluster, submit the job to This Computer, and allow Compressor to harness any unmanaged services, all of the processors (cores) that you've made available will be tasked to the job.

To create a virtual cluster, follow the steps in "Setting Up the Node Computer" to configure your system as an unmanaged node with available service instances. Also ensure that the target has Job Segmenting enabled (see "Submitting a Batch to a QuickCluster").

When submitting a batch, select the "Include unmanaged services on other computers" checkbox.

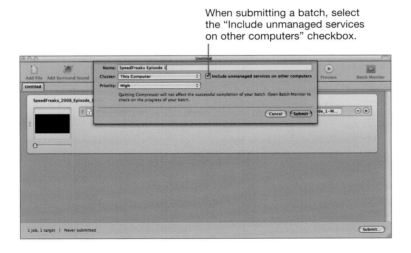

Compressor will then capture all of the available local services as if they were nodes on the network. In this example, four services were created from eight cores.

You can also create a QuickCluster within your local computer to have, in essence, a single system that acts as both controller and node. Follow the steps above for creating a QuickCluster by choosing "QuickCluster with services" from the Qmaster pane and select the Managed checkbox for the Compressor service. Submit batches to your local QuickCluster

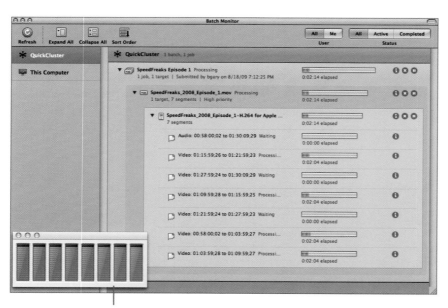

This is the floating CPU window from Activity Monitor. Notice that all eight cores are processing the job.

NOTE ▶ Local clusters can have very high hardware requirements because each service must have full RAM available to it as if it were a stand-alone computer—meaning that if a node requires 2 GB of RAM, then four instances in a local cluster would require 8 GB of RAM.

Technical Considerations

Distributed processing in Compressor adds a layer of technical complexity to the process of encoding media. Use the following table to guide you when submitting encoding jobs to a virtual or remote cluster.

Codec	Distributed Processing Considerations
AIC, Apple ProRes	These codecs are multi-threaded and will take advantage of all available processors (cores). There is no minimum clip duration for job segmenting.
MPEG-2	This codec is multi-threaded. The best performance for local clusters will be achieved when using half of the available services. For example, on an eight-core machine, use four services.
H.264	This codec is not multi-threaded. You must have job segmenting enabled for this codec to take advantage of distributed processing. The minimum clip duration for segmenting is two minutes. Note: Using H.264 encoding for Blu-ray does not take advantage of distributed encoding, and the "Allow Job Segmenting" option is dimmed in the Encoder pane of those targets.
Any codec used in an Episode custom setting	The Episode workflow in Compressor does not take advantage of distributed processing. You will need to use the proprietary Episode Engine as an alternative to Apple Qmaster. Refer to the Episode documentation for more information.

NOTE ▶ For more information on distributed processing, visit the Compressor website (www.apple.com/finalcutstudio/compressor).

To evaluate your understanding of the concepts covered in this lesson and to prepare for the Apple Pro Certification Exam, download the online quiz at www.peachpit.com/apts.compressor.

Glossary

1:37:1 Aspect ratio of 35mm film, commonly referred to as *Academy ratio*.

1:85:1 Widescreen version of the Academy aspect ratio.

2:35:1 Aspect ratio common to widescreen, theatrical release motion pictures.

3:2 Aspect ratio common to digital video (DV) and DVD.

3:2 pulldown A process for converting film footage frame rates to video-footage frame rates. Also referred to as a 2:3 pulldown.

4:3 Aspect ratio of a standard definition NTSC television set.

16:9 Aspect ratio of a television set and HD video formats. Also referred to as 1:78:1.

16-bit A standard bit depth for digital audio recording and playback.

alpha channel A channel that exists in some file formats along with the color channels. Used to store transparency information for compositing purposes. Formats that support an alpha channel include Targa, TIFF, PICT, PSD, and the QuickTime Animation codec.

AppleScript Scripting language developed by Apple Computer that sends commands to scriptable applications and creates simple instruction sets that can be packaged into executable files.

aspect ratio The ratio of the width and height of an image. For example, standard definition TV has an aspect ratio of 4:3; high-definition TV has a 16:9 aspect ratio.

bandwidth A measurement of the amount of data delivered from a source to a destination within a period of time. Generally stated in kilobits per second (kbps) or megabits per second (Mbps).

bit budgeting The process of calculating the required data rates of media to determine if that media will fit within a specific bandwidth or within the storage limitations of a distribution format.

bit rate (also *bitrate*) A measurement of the quantity of data transmitted over time. See also *bandwidth*.

Blu-ray Disc A high-density (up to 50 GB) optical media format that can hold data, SD video, and HD video.

chroma sampling The process of storing more luminance information relative to the color information in a video signal. Commonly represented as a ratio of three numbers, such as 4:2:2 or 4:4:4, where the first number represents the luminance value, and the next two numbers represent the color values.

codec Abbreviation for *compression/decompression*. A program used to compress and decompress data such as audio and video files.

compression A process by which data files (often video, graphics, and audio data) are reduced in size. Size reduction of an audio or video file that is implemented by removing perceptually-redundant image data is referred to as *lossy* compression. *Lossless* compression uses a mathematical process to reduce file size by consolidating redundant information without discarding it. wSee also *codec*.

D

data rate The speed at which data is transferred, often described in megabytes per second (Mbps). Higher video data rates usually exhibit increased visual quality, but higher data rates also require more system resources (such as processor speed and hard disk space) for processing. Some codecs allow you to specify a maximum data rate for a media capture. See also *bandwidth, bit rate.*

deinterlace Combining video frames composed of two interlaced fields into a single unified frame.

demux (demultiplex) Process of separating combined audio and video files into separate elementary streams.

digital intermediate (DI) High-resolution digital media created from film footage for the purpose of color correction and other creative picture adjustments.

DPX Still image file format for digital intermediate and digital effects work.

F

field dominance The choice of whether field 1 or field 2 will first be displayed on a monitor. The default value should be lower (field 2) for DV and Targa captures.

floating point A system of calculation that allows otherwise fixed incremental measurements within a bit depth to change in relative fashion so that a higher degree of accuracy can be achieved at the widest dynamic ranges.

frame rate The playback speed of individual images in a moving sequence, either film or video, measured in frames per second (fps). Film in 16mm or 35mm is usually shot at 24 fps; NTSC video at 29.97 fps; and PAL video at 25 fps. HD content can employ a variety of frame rates depending on the format.

H

HD (high definition) Formats created to increase the number of pixels (resolution) of video images, and to solve many of the frame rate and cadence problems that exist between film and video. The two most common pixel resolutions for HD footage are 1080 with a native resolution of 1920 x 1080; and 720 with a native resolution of 1280 x 720. Both formats can be recorded at various frame rates and can be interlaced or progressive.

H.264/AVC/MPEG-2 Part 10 Advanced codec that employs block-oriented, motion-compensated compression. Widely used in both distribution and acquisition formats.

I

I frame See *keyframe.*

interlaced video A video scanning method that first scans odd-numbered picture lines (field 1) and then scans the even-numbered picture lines (field 2). The two fields are combined to constitute a single frame of video.

K

keyframe (also *I frame*) A frame encoded with the entire image data and no reference to any other frame. In intraframe compression, all frames are keyframes. In interframe compression, an interval of keyframes is separated by delta frames that interpolate their image data by referencing multiple keyframes.

L

lossless compression See *compression.*

lossy compression See *compression.*

metadata Information in a digital file that includes additional data in the content or context of the media.

MPEG (Moving Pictures Experts Group) A group of compression standards for video and audio developed by that group, which includes MPEG-1, MPEG-2, MPEG-1 Layer 3 (MP3), and MPEG-4.

multiplexed (also *muxing*) The interleaving of audio and video into one stream.

muxing See *multiplexed.*

M

NTSC (National Television Systems Committee) A standard format for color TV broadcasting developed by the committee and used mainly in North America, Mexico, and Japan. The NTSC format consists of 525 scan lines per frame of 720 x 486 pixel resolution (720 x 480 for DV), running at a 29.97 fps rate.

N

PAL (phase alternating line) A color TV broadcasting standard used primarily in Europe and consisting of 625 lines per frame of 720 x 546 pixel resolution, and running at a 25 fps rate.

P

pixel Abbreviation for *picture element*. One dot in a digital video or still image.

pixel aspect ratio The width-to-height ratio for the pixels that compose an image. Pixels on computer screens and in high-definition video signals are square (1:1 ratio); pixels in standard-definition video signals are not square (0.9:1 ratio).

progressive frame video (also *progressive scan*) A format for delivering video in which all lines are drawn in sequence. Its presence is commonly denoted by the letter *p*, such as *720p* or *1080p*.

progressive scan See *progressive frame video.*

RGB (red-green-blue) The three primary colors that make up a color video image.

R

sample rate The frequency at which analog audio is measured and converted into digital data. The sampling rate of an audio stream specifies how often digital samples are captured. Higher sample rates yield higher-quality audio. Standard audio sampling rates are usually measured in kilohertz (kHz). The standard CD sampling rate is 44.1 kHz. A rate of 48 kHz is also common in professional audio production.

S

SD (standard definition) The term used to differentiate traditional television resolutions from those of the high-definition formats. Standard-definition resolutions are 720 x 486 (NTSC) or 720 x 576 (PAL). See also *HD.*

Transcode Process of converting media from one format to another format. Closely related to encode but with the connotation of a lateral move in quality.

T

telecine The process of transferring film footage to video media. Can also refer to the machine that performs the process.

TIFF (tagged image file format) A bitmapped graphics file format for monochrome, grayscale, and 8- and 24-bit color images. There are two types of TIFF images: with an alpha channel and without an alpha channel.

timecode A numbering system of electronic signals placed onto video content and used to identify individual video frames. Each video frame is labeled with hours, minutes, seconds, and frames, expressed in the format: 01:00:00:00. Timecode can be drop frame, non-drop frame, time of day (TOD), or EBU (European Broadcast Union) for PAL projects.

Xsan Apple Computer's branded, cross-platform SAN (storage area network) solution that offers both high speed and large storage capacity.

X

YUV The three-channel PAL video signal with one luminance (Y) and two chrominance color difference signals (UV).

Y

Index

Apple Certification
Fuel your mind.
Reach your potential.

Stand out from the crowd. Differentiate yourself and gain recognition for your expertise by earning Apple Certified Pro status to validate your Compressor 3.5 skills.

How to Earn Apple Certified Pro Status

As a special offer to owners of *Compressor 3.5,* you are eligible to take the certification exam online for $75.00 USD. Normally you must pay to take the exam in a proctored setting at an Apple Authorized Training Center (AATC). To take the exam, please follow these steps:

1 Log on to ibt.prometric/apple, click Secure Sign-In (uses SSL encryption) and enter your Prometric Prime ID. If you don't have an ID, click First-Time Registration to create one.

2 Click Continue to verify your information.

3 In the Candidate Menu page, click Change Domain on the left and set the Domain to IT&ProApps.

4 Click Take Test.

5 Enter CompEUPP in the Private Tests box and click Submit. The codes are case sensitive and are only valid for one use.

6 Click Take This Test, then Continue to skip the voucher and enter your credit card information to pay the $75 USD fee.

7 Click Begin Test at the bottom of the page.

8 When you finish, click End Test. If you do not pass, retake instructions are included in the results email, so do not discard this email. Retakes are also $75.

Reasons to Become an Apple Certified Pro

- **Raise your earning potential.** Studies show that certified professionals can earn more than their non-certified peers.

- **Distinguish yourself from others in your industry.** Proven mastery of an application helps you stand out from the crowd.

- **Publicize your Apple Certifications.** Each certification provides a logo to display on business cards, resumes and websites. In addition, you can publish your certifications on the Apple Certified Professionals Registry to connect with schools, clients and employers.

Training Options

Apple's comprehensive curriculum addresses your needs, whether you're an IT or creative professional, educator, or service technician. Hands-on training is available through a worldwide network of Apple Authorized Training Centers (AATCs) or in a self-paced format through the Apple Training Series and Apple Pro Training Series. Learn more about Apple's curriculum and find an AATC near you at training.apple.com.

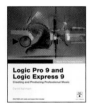